This book is dedicated to:

KIRSTIN

Our grandchild, already a book-lover, aged three,
whose arrival has brightened our lives.

JOHN BUNYAN
PRISONER FOR CHRIST

John Bunyan
PRISONER FOR CHRIST

BY

GEORGE J. MITCHELL

AMBASSADOR INTERNATIONAL
Greenville, South Carolina • Belfast, Northern Ireland

John Bunyan:
Prisoner for Christ

Cover design & page layout by A & E Media — Paula Shepherd

ISBN 1 932307 28 1

Published by the Ambassador Group

Ambassador Emerald International
427 Wade Hampton Blvd.
Greenville, SC 29609
USA
www.emeraldhouse.com

and

Ambassador Publications Ltd.
Providence House
Ardenlee Street
Belfast BT6 8QJ
Northern Ireland
www.ambassador-productions.com

The colophon is a trademark of Ambassador

TABLE OF CONTENTS

ACKNOWLEDGMENTS

Once again, we say, I owe so much to so many people in my Christian pilgrimage, that I had better restrict my thanks to this task. I am very grateful to Bible teachers and leaders, like Jack Brown, Roy Miller and Isa Calder who first introduced me to John Bunyan. I also want to thank Samuel Lowry and Ambassador Productions for their help, encouragement and expertise in this project. Derick Bingham has also helped to jolly me along as a Christian writer.

I would like to thank the Principal and Staff, especially Gwenda Bond, the Librarian, for the use of the library of International Christian College, Glasgow, and the ever-helpful Staff of the Mitchell Library, Glasgow. Drs Jim Blair and Shirley Carr have given good advice in medical matters, and Fraser Copeland in the book-lending department.

I enjoyed meeting my fellow-writers through their work, especially Christopher Hill and Vera Britten.

Many thanks also to Mhairi and Laura Jack, discerning and cool sisters who live in our street, for casting a critical eye over the work.

I am in debt again to my wife Jean, whose secretarial help and practical advice are greatly valued. I pray that God will use this book to bless, encourage and challenge all who read it—especially today's boys and girls!

INTRODUCTION

I first met John Bunyan, so to speak, in the back hall of Lambhill Evangelistic Mission, Glasgow, where I attended the Intermediate Christian Endeavour Society meeting. Around fifteen teenagers sat spellbound as our vigorous leader, Jack Brown, in his big deep voice went through the story of 'Pilgrim's Progress' in weekly episodes, with a weekly 'cliff-hanger.'

Ever since those wonderful days, the wide variety of events concerning the penniless tinker-turned-preacher have fascinated me. I have felt that I have met many of the characters described in 'Pilgrim's Progress.' As a preacher I have used many of the people and incidents from Bunyan's books for the last forty years. When telling people about Jesus dying on the Cross, I have often used Pilgrim's speech:

> *'Thus far did I come, laden with my sin,*
> *Nor could aught ease the grief that I was in,*
> *Till I came hither. What a place is this!*
> *Must here be the beginning of my bliss?*

Must here the burdens fall from off my back?
Must here the thongs that bound me to it crack?
Blest Cross! Blest Sepulchre! Blest rather be,
The Man that there was put to shame for me!'

I have often thought that the Lord has a sense of humour. It is funny that Bunyan has become an attractive figure in the town where so many despised and rejected him, and that many books have been written about his life and work. (I think that happened to Someone else, didn't it?)

As I have written about Bunyan, I have felt like someone who has been allowed to put his toe in the shallow end of an Olympic-size swimming pool, aware of the depths (of scholarship) within my reach. As in so many fields of study, the books laugh from the shelves at the would-be scholar, in Bunyan's case more than eight hundred of them! I hope that my puny efforts to make the story of Bunyan's life and work simple enough for young people to understand may have some measure of success. My aim is that today's children and young people might be inspired to love and serve the Lord Jesus as a result of reading my story about this Christian 'tinker and thinker'. John Bunyan is the kind of person who has 'kept up the rumour that God is not dead.'

chapter one

MISSING ANDY...

Amy Taylor closed the outside door a bit more firmly than usual, flung her books on the settee, and flopped into her favourite armchair. With a toss of her head, her auburn curls cascaded over the back of the chair.

'Had a good day, dear?' her Mum asked, heavily, in her 'silly voice', as Amy called it.

'I think you know the answer to that question', Amy replied.

'Well, who was rattling your cage today?'—'was it Miss PE, Mr. RE or Mr. History?'

'It WAS Mr. Hamilton, o.k.a Mr. History' Amy responded. 'He was banging on about some old guy called John Bunyan, and his famous book 'Pilgrim's Progress'. I've never even heard of him, or his book.' Whoever he is, we won't escape him, for Mr. History says he's an inter-disciplinary study, and is liable to rear his ugly head in English, History, Drama and Religious Education. Why should he have a place in the National Curriculum? And how did he get that funny name?

Amy's Mum spoke steadily and seriously. 'John Bunyan was one of England's finest Christians and writers, Amy, but we'll talk about that later...Anything else to report?'

'You know Andy Burnett, the boy from our church who sat at the same table in our classroom in Junior school? It's very sad, Mum, but he's to be at home all the time now. He is ill with cystic fibrosis, and it seems to have knocked him flat.'

'I'm sorry to hear that, Amy, because he seemed a very bright boy.'

'Bright?' said Amy. 'He's brilliant! He seems to be a computer whiz-kid. Remember all the info he got us on the Dinosaur project? Some of the boys call him 'Brains' Burnett. He's what they call a 'polymath' He is the 'man who knows' in the class. He can find out anything about anything—sport, science, history, computing—and he's not big-headed! I remember that he promised anyone whose question he couldn't answer right away, that he would answer it the next day—but refused to tell anyone where he found the answer! He is the 'Man who knows but will not tell how he gets to know.'

'He can also write very funny poems, invent brilliant nick-names, and tell some very funny jokes. Although he's never in good health, he's a smiler, and his sayings keep us all smiling. When he is off-guard, we can see that he is sometimes in pain. He keeps using a pile of names and sayings no-one else uses, like: 'you're not often right, but you're wrong again!', 'in the

name of Pharaoh', 'Patrice Lumumba!' 'hoi polloi!', 'jumpin'
stuff!', or 'a clever Alsatian (dog) could do that!' It's a pity for
him and us that he won't be around school very much. At best,
he'll only be there for short periods of time.'

Fiona Taylor, Amy's Mum, had noticed Andy around at
church events. Although he was barely a teenager, there was
a maturity about him which protected him from bitterness or
cruelty. Although his physical limitations were obvious to most
people, he made light of them in a way that won sympathy and
respect. His dark eyes took in everything around him. Fiona
went into thoughtful mode before replying to Amy. 'Amy, I
wonder if we could make the best of this situation. You are
a bright twelve-year-old, and he probably would like to have
some young company of his own age. He's probably trying
hard to settle into working at home, but you know how he
loves to get his teeth into some project. Maybe he needs to have
something to keep the little grey cells in his brain busy. Why
not visit him, and see how you get on? Why don't you ask for
his help about John Bunyan, and cheer him up? If you get on
well, it may turn into a weekly visit. The only problem is I don't
know what your class-mates will say if they find out. You know
that lot can spot a romance a mile away!'

Amy thought for a minute before she spoke. 'Who cares?
You're right, Mum. Remember your saying 'Who says? What
do they say? Let them say...' Andy's a good pal and I bet he's
still fascinating to listen to. I'll just do that!'

Fiona said: 'It's only fair to warn you that cystic fibrosis
is a distressing thing to watch as it gets worse. The medical

people call it a degenerative disease. The sufferers need a lot of attention, pills, and physical help. You may get a shock when you see Andy....'

Amy got things going by phoning Andy's Mum, and setting up her subject-matter by telling Andy about her search for information about John Bunyan.

chapter two

WHO WAS JOHN BUNYAN?

Amy was not a football fan like her brother Robert, so she thought Saturday afternoon was a good time to visit Andy. She phoned to make sure, and then headed for Andy's home, a three-bedroom semi-detached house in the better part of Leahaven, the seaside town where they lived.

Amy was busy with her internal check-list, as she took an inventory of Andy's area. 'Welcome to Legoland! Nice street, good house, trimmed hedge, the kind of garden in which no weed was allowed peace to grow, colourful well-stocked garden beds, bright but not gaudy curtains, modern glass front door with stained-glass galleon in the centre panel, good loud door-bell'...(Amy hated those door-bells which either didn't work, or left you wondering whether they did or not).

'Amy! This is good of you to come! Andy's looking forward to seeing you. Come on in, and I'll take you upstairs.' The whole house seemed amazingly light and airy. Full-length

windows at the front and sliding patio doors at the back fixed
that impression downstairs, and the impression persisted as
they made their way upstairs, past a large window on the half-
landing. Amy was surprised at the size of Andy's bedroom,
the middle bedroom in the three-bedroom semi. Andy's
room was a battleground of smells. A sanitised, hospital
odour of carbolic fought against the fragrance of flower-
scented air fresheners. Bookshelves surrounded Andy's bed
like soldiers on guard, and had attempted a take-over on the
other walls. A singing, dancing, state-of-the-art computer
with the full range of accessories filled the computer desk in
the corner. The bookshelves were stuffed with no-nonsense
reference books and the desk held racks of CDs loaded with
information. Opposite the window, Andy was propped up in
bed with pillows, like a melting snowman surrounded with
marshmallow. Amy's gaze took in the shock of black hair, and
Andy's tiny but neat ears. Amy remembered her Mum's warning
about his condition as an accurate prediction. He looked pale,
and his body seemed smaller, but his head and face seemed
larger and puffier, and the circles under his eyes seemed larger
and darker. 'Must be the tablets he's taking', Amy thought.
Andy gave her a great welcome, swept aside her enquiries about
his health, and launched into his subject immediately.

'Great to see you, Amy! A friend in need is a pest!—only
teasing!

Now—John Bunyan! The Americans would call him
awesome and mega! Fit as a flea, with a mind like a razor!
Did you know that over eight hundred books have been

written about him? He is the focus for scholarly circles all over the world. His book 'Pilgrim's Progress', which he wrote in prison, has been translated into umpteen languages, and is second only to the Bible in world-wide sales. He had very little formal education. Yet the humble tinker has become a major tourist attraction in the district of Bedford, which would have been a bit of puzzle or an embarrassment to some of the rich and famous folk of his day if they knew about it. They called him 'that tinker', and he became so unpopular with the mainstream church leaders and authorities, that he spent over twelve years in prison in Bedford.

'Have you found out anything about the name Bunyan, Andy? It sounds like a sore foot.'

'Well, since you got me involved in this detective hunt, you'll have to listen' said Andy. There are connections with bunions! The Old French 'buignon' describes any mass or gathering of material, like a raised 'bun' with a fruit centre, a 'bunch' of flowers, or a raised swelling on the foot, like a 'bunion'. John Bunyan's father seems to be the first to give the name the form we know, although there were thirty-four different versions of it.

Your pal John Bunyan lays a bit of a false trail for amateur detectives like me. He describes his family background in his book 'Grace Abounding to the Chief of Sinners' like this: 'My father's house being of that rank that is meanest and most despised of all the families in the land...so I cannot, as some others can, boast of noble blood and the high-born state'. He may have been truly humble and wanted to understate the case, and/or truly keen to 'talk up' the work of God in his life, but his description is a bit misleading.'

'How do you know that?' Amy reacted to Andy's statement of the case.

'Well', Andy coughed and then continued, 'there are all these versions of the name Bunyan, for starters. The name is known in the Bedfordshire district from the twelfth century, and its French connections may mean the family came over to England soon after William the Conqueror's success in A.D.1066. The name would not be used so often unless the family was well-established. As well as that, John Bunyan's father and grandfather had wills witnessed. Admittedly, they signed 'with their mark', probably an 'X' or a thumbprint, because they couldn't write, but folk who were really poor never made wills. A detective hunt through the local courts shows that the story of the Bunyans is that of a family gradually selling off their land assets as the generations passed. John's grandfather Thomas sold land, bringing the family down to nine acres, and when he died in 1641, he left John 6d! John's father was also called Thomas, and although the area was known as 'Bonyon's End', he was so poor that his one-hearthed cottage at Harrowden was exempted from hearth-tax in 1673-4.

Amy sat up and took more notice, asking: 'What did the Bunyans do for a living, Andy? And how do you know all this?'

'I'll answer your first question first,' Andy replied. 'They were probably smallholders at first, perhaps linked to the work of the Nunnery, which was founded soon after the Norman

Conquest. (a Nunnery is a centre for nuns, holy women who are sometimes cruelly nicknamed 'birds of pray'). The Bunyans sold off bits of land during the reigns of Henry VIII and Elizabeth, and Thomas, the great-great-grandfather of John was described in 1542 as 'a victualler, common brewer of beer.' John's grandfather Thomas was called a 'brazier' (worker in brass) and 'petty chapman' (pedlar, or door-to-door salesman). When John grew up, he followed his father's trade as a 'braseyer' (brazier) 'tinker'.

'What did a tinker do?' asked Amy.

'The description 'tinker' is linked with gypsies in Scotland, but in England it generally means someone who is a skilled metal-worker who travels to repair metal objects.

'I'm beginning to feel a little tired, so we'll talk about tinkers on your next visit.'

'Now, in answer to your second question about how I know all this—that would be telling!

'Jumpin' stuff! As you would say yourself, Andy,' Amy interrupted. Kindly get off your technical bandwagon, Andy, and tell me a little more about the family before I go.'

'Amy, sadly, in those days, women lived for a much shorter time than men, mainly due to death while giving birth to babies, and the complications which followed, in the absence of disinfectants and anaesthetics. John Bunyan's grandfather had four wives, his father had three, and John Bunyan himself had two. At least four of his grandfather's children died as infants, as did John's step-brother Charles. John Bunyan's mother, an Elstow girl, was his father's second wife. John had a younger sister called Margaret, born in 1630 and a younger brother William, born three years later.'

Andy suddenly turned pale, and gave a tired sigh. 'I'm really sorry, Amy, but I'll have to ask you to leave. It was really marvellous of you to give up your time to come and visit me. Please, please come back soon—it would be great to see you. It's just too bad that you are interrupting 'punching time!' My Mum gets withdrawal symptoms if she goes too long without pummelling my ribs,' he said with a kind of tired twinkle...

Andy waved weakly, and said 'See you soon!'

chapter three

JOHN BUNYAN—THE BOY

As soon as Amy closed the door behind her, her Mum was 'on the job' of interrogation right away, keen to know how she got on. 'I had a good time, Mum, and Andy and his family were very welcoming. But he looks worse than I remember, and he tired fairly quickly. Mind you, he has been very busy already, and what he knows about Bunyan is amazing for someone who stays at home and lets his fingers do the walking. Mum, could you tell me a bit more about this cystic fibrosis?'

'Well, Amy, until a few years ago, this was a killer disease, and most people with the disease didn't live beyond their teens. 'CF' is an inherited or genetic condition that affects the glands which produce mucus, tears, sweat, saliva and the digestive juices. Normally these secretions are good lubricants, thin and slippery, but in CF a defective gene makes these secretions thick and sticky. They clog up the patient's tubes, ducts and passageways, especially in the pancreas and lungs. The most dangerous aspect of CF tends to be respiratory failure (loss of breath). The disease is much more common among white babies than among black or Asian children. I'll tell you more later, if you want to know.'

'What did Andy mean when he spoke about his Mum pummelling his ribs?' asked Amy.

'People with CF need a way to physically remove thick mucus from their lungs, by coughing it up. This is often done by manually clapping on the front and back of their chest. Sometimes an electric chest clapper, known as a mechanical percussor, is used. Patients need bronchial airway drainage for twenty to thirty minutes twice a day...Older children and adults can learn to do this without going outside the family.'

'Should I go back? Isn't it too much for Andy?' Amy asked.

'Please, please go back, and keep going' Mum said. 'Andy loves to meet people and behave as normally as possible. His Mum told me he is so pleased you asked for his help, and loves ferreting out information for you.'

The following Saturday was one of those days when you wonder just how much rain is stored in the clouds. The steady drumbeat of raindrops kept Amy indoors all morning. In the afternoon, she made a break for it, and escaped to visit Andy.

'Hullo, hullo! Are you back to hear more about the Tink from the Clink?!'

Amy went straight into action. 'Be careful, Andy, or they'll cart you off. Giving that title to John Bunyan is insulting to tinkers and is probably unacceptable to the European Commission! You were going to tell us more about tinkers anyway, but where does 'the clink' fit in?'

'I'm glad you asked that,' said Andy as his Mum puffed up his pillows, knowing that the Brain was about to launch into one of his lengthy explanations. 'You see, as I told you last time, a tinker was a skilled metal-worker, who travelled to repair metal objects, especially tin ones. He worked from house to house, or in country areas like Bedfordshire, from farm to farm. When John Bunyan was a small boy, he would be able to watch his Dad working at home, because a tinker would often have a small forge in a lean-to alongside his house, and did some of his work at home. A tinker would usually carry a bag of tools with him on his travels, including a light anvil, and portable bellows, to do on-the-spot repairs. The tinker was skilful in the heat treatment of metals like tin, and alloys (metal mixtures) like pewter, which was a tin/lead alloy, with no more than 20% lead, used mainly for tankards. Tinkers also used solder to repair leaky pots, pans and utensils, as well as using engineering skills to repair, sharpen and service agricultural machinery. They would heat up charcoal with bellows, and generate high enough temperatures to soften or melt solid metals into liquid, so that they could use their skills to mix the metals. All of this must have seemed like magic to children, who are always interested in fires and forges. You can imagine small groups of boys and girls gathering to watch the tinker at work. John Bunyan must have been fascinated by all this from his youngest days.'

'In the English language, tinkers were ridiculed for their low status ('as worthless as a tinker's curse'), their unsocial behaviour (as drunk/quarrelsome as a tinker), and for some of them, their bad craftsmanship led to the use of the term 'to tinker', meaning to interfere with in a ham-fisted, amateurish way.'

'Andy, as the Americans say, you sure done slobbered a bibful there,' said Amy, 'But why 'the clink?'

'There was a prison called the Clink, in the Southwark area of London, and because of the noise made by prison doors and prisoners' chains rattling, it came to be used as a slang term for prison. John Bunyan the tinker spent over twelve years in 'clink' when he was a grown-up. I'll tell you why later!'

'I can't wait!' said Amy with a hint of playfulness, 'but what can you tell us about John Bunyan the Boy?'

'He was born in the village of Elstow, about a mile-and-a-half from Bedford, and was baptized 'John, the sonne of Thomas Bonnion Junr' on 30th November 1628, joining the names of seventeen other babies in the parish records for that year. His mother's maiden name was Margaret Bentley, a family of 'decent and worthy ways', according to John Bunyan. Margaret Bentley's mother, widow of William Bentley, left a will giving her daughter Margaret 'the joined stools in the chamber.' They were a family of sufficient status to make a will, but materially poor.'

'Did John Bunyan go to school?' Amy asked.

'Many village children were illiterate, but we know that John Bunyan had some basic education. We don't know which school he attended, or how long he went there. He thanked God later for 'putting it into the hearts of my parents to put me to school to learn both to read and write.' Elsewhere he wrote: 'I never went to school to Aristotle or Plato, but was brought up at my father's house in a very mean condition.' He also said

'I did soon lose that little I learned, long before the Lord did His gracious work of conversion upon my soul.'

John probably attended either the Free School at Houghton Conquest, about three miles south west of Elstow on the road to Ampthill, founded by Sir Francis Clark, or the former Grammar School at Bedford, founded in 1566 by Sir William Harpur for 'poor boys of the town to learn grammar and good manners.' The county town has four Harpur Trust schools today. Both local schools had a blemished record for over-charging, neglect and cruelty. Some scholars think John Bunyan may have learned a little Latin later on, although Charles Doe describes him as 'a very profane sinner, and an illiterate man.'

'As we noted earlier, Thomas Bunyan, John's father was a poor man with a one-hearthed house, so it would probably be cold in the winter, and first up would be best-dressed. Bedford was a sleepy town, and Elstow was a village surrounded by fields. Links with London and the surrounding towns were poor, and the road system was a disgrace. The red-letter time in the calendar for Elstow was a three-day fair on the village green, beside the Moot House, in May every year. This brought in customers from far and near, and brought the community its annual thrill. John Bunyan based his description of Vanity Fair in his book 'Pilgrim's Progress' on this event.

'What were the main influences on the life of Bunyan as a boy?' Amy asked.

'His father Thomas had a foul tongue—he cursed his way through life and blasphemed (used the names of God and

Jesus as if they were swear words) every time he spoke. His son John caught this habit, and swore like a tinker, and later a trooper, as he grew up.

John would take the usual country boy's interest in butterflies, dragonflies and birds, note the changing of the seasons, watch the flowers, gathered hips and haws, and collected tadpoles and newts, and would be generally thrilled with the life of the land. He was a bit of a dare-devil. He once narrowly escaped drowning. Another time, he stunned an adder with a stick, with which he opened its mouth and removed the sting with his fingers, which was highly dangerous. He would enter into the cut-and-thrust of children's games, and develop his skills at the games that the adults played in the village.'

'What grown-up games did John like?' asked Amy.

'His four favourites were 'tip-cat', tree-climbing, dancing and bell-ringing.'

'Tip-cat sounds suspiciously like cruelty to animals,' said Amy. 'What was that game all about?'

'It was a very skilful game,' Andy replied. 'I've just discovered that it has been registered recently as an official sport in America.' Andy glowed so much with discovery at his recently-acquired knowledge, that Amy wanted to punch him...'Boys are impossible!' she muttered under her breath.

He continued: 'The 'cat' was a piece of wood about 6-8 inches in total length, shaped as a cylinder in the centre with a cone shaped at each end. The player struck, or 'tipped' the cat at one end with a stick or bat, so that it flew up from the ground, and then the player struck it again in mid-air for as far as he could hit it. Players ran round a series of bases, with rules for elimination for the runners and points-scoring for the batsmen rather like baseball or rounders. Tip-cat demanded very good hand-to-eye-co-ordination, physical strength, and running power. As a small boy, John Bunyan would be mesmerised as he watched the adults playing tip-cat, and his longings to be a good player were fulfilled as he grew into a husky teenager and expert player, tipping the cat with animal ferocity.'

'Where's the skill in tree-climbing?' Amy asked, with a quizzical look on her face.

'Are you serious?' Andy replied. 'Have you ever climbed a tree? Tree-climbing was also a physically demanding sport, and Elstow had its own village legends about the exploits of the villagers over the years.'

'I suppose,' Amy conceded 'tree climbers would have to conquer their self-preservation instinct, and become risk-takers and dare-devils.' 'It's easier to be a tree-hugger than a tree-climber!'

'Got it in one, Amy,' agreed Andy.

'Would dancing in Bunyan's time be anything like dancing as we know it, or would it be like the Morris dancing we sometimes see demonstrated at holiday resorts? Amy asked.

'Well, I suppose there would be a back-to-nature, slap-stick, round-the-maypole kind of dancing,' Andy said. Then he blushed as he explained to Amy that dancing has always been part of training for social skills that boys and girls acquire as part of growing up, and here the 'contact sport' element came in, without becoming like the cheek-to-cheek smooching of the present day.

'Let's hurry on to bell-ringing, Andy,' Amy said, smiling as she sensed his awkwardness, 'since dancing seems to be a sensitive area!'

'Oh, you mean Campanology,' Andy grinned and tossed his head in an artificial manner.

'Well, Professor Peanut, I suppose you know all about that as well! Go on, enlighten our darkened thoughts! Write indelibly on the empty blackboard of our minds!'

Andy took a deep breath, and launched himself into one of his extended explanations.

'Campanology is the art or study of bell-ringing. It gets its name from Campania, an area of Southern Italy near Naples, where there were lots of factories and foundries, and where bells were produced.'

'A Campanile is a bell-tower, usually attached to a church or civic building in Britain, but often free-standing on the Continent. The Leaning Tower of Pisa, for example, is a Campanile. The bell tower at Elstow stands apart from the church building, and is a Campanile.'

'Sorry for teasing you, Andy,' Amy interrupted. 'How do they make bells?'

'It's the appliance of science, Amy.' Andy continued: 'Bell metal is an alloy of copper and tin, with small amounts of zinc and lead. Big bells contain less tin (about 20%) than small bells (about 25%), because tin increases brittleness. The bell founders of the Chou Dynasty (1125-221 BC) were superb craftsmen in Ancient China. The best founders in Western Europe lived in Belgium and the Netherlands (for example, the Hemony Brothers, 17th century AD experts).

'Bells were generally cup-shaped with a flared opening and an internal clapper, producing on impact a ringing sound through the vibration of resonant metal in the sound bow, or bulge, near the rim. The liquid metal poured into bell moulds reached 1100 degrees Celsius or 2000 degrees Fahrenheit, and required up to two weeks of patient and careful cooling to prevent stress fractures (cracking) in the bell's later life. Bells have a complex acoustical structure—a single bell tolls, two free-swinging bells peal, and at least 23 bells are called a carillon.'

'Where did John Bunyan fit into all this?' Amy asked.

'Elstow had a fine bell-tower, with teams ringing 5 to 12 bells in mathematical permutations. When he became an adult, he became bell-rope Number 4. As a small boy, John became fascinated with this habit, and was obsessed with the skill attached to it, and acquired it himself. This helped him to develop his own physical strength. Theologically, if you'll pardon the joke, it rang a few bells for him, and had a few religious overtones.'

'What were they?' Amy asked with a puzzled look

'Although bells weren't used in Christian churches until the sixth century AD, legends persisted about their special powers, which affected John Bunyan from the time he was a small boy. Bells weren't just used for signalling, to call people to church, or announce special events. Many people believed they could start off thunderstorms, dispel demons, invoke curses and lift spells. Bells have often been used as war trophies, or patriotic symbols, like the Liberty Bell in America. That is why bells are worn as fashion accessories, like amulets or in charm bracelets.'

Suddenly, Andy became pale with his exertions, and Amy realised it was time to go home.

Andy waved a tired good-bye.

'Don't forget Professor Peanut' he said. 'He really appreciates your visits. Come again soon.'

chapter four

THE BOY LEAVES HOME

Amy returned from Andy's house, opened the front door, and rushed headlong into her mother's arms. Amy started to sob and cry.

'What's wrong, Amy?' her Mum said to her, tenderly.

'Mum, I was just thinking on the way home about the terrible waste of a brilliant mind in a decaying body. It reminded me of an episode on Star Trek on TV, of a decaying race of very clever aliens imprisoned in decaying bodies. Mum, how long is Andy likely to live?'

'Amy, I'm sorry to say that the best we can hope for under present circumstances is until his thirties. That is a big improvement on twenty years ago, and modern medicine has given CF sufferers fuller and more comfortable lives. The other thing is that genetics is an area of medicine where there are several new advances, and we hope and pray that a cure would come soon.'

'Andy is so clever and patient with his illness,' said Amy. 'He doesn't complain, and he seems to make little of the pain he's going through.'

'Yes, he is a brave lad, Amy.' Her Mum sighed. 'I suppose his positive approach is the best approach, and the best thing you can do for him is to be his friend. Amy, you must promise me that if it becomes too much for you, then you'll have to stop visiting.'

'Alright, Mum, but he seems to enjoy the visits, and he seems to be increasingly interested in our pal John Bunyan. I must say I have appreciated his help when we tackle this subject at school.'

The following Saturday, Amy breezed into Andy's room, and found him more than ready to answer all her questions.

'Andy, tell me what England was like when John Bunyan was a child.'

'John Bunyan's century, the seventeenth, saw the only Civil War in England in the whole of her history, and the only execution of one of her kings.'

The Stuart Kings were fairly unpopular with the English people. They propagated the doctrine of the divine right of kings, arguing from texts like Romans 13 verse 1 in the New Testament : 'The powers that be are ordained by God' The first king in the dynasty, James I, had been king of Scotland as James VI, and reigned over the dual monarchy until his death in 1625. He was a bizarre individual with some odd habits. He wore thickly padded jackets in case someone tried to stab him, and he liked to shout (and spit!) into his courtiers' faces....John Bunyan's life straddles some of the biggest crises in the seventeenth century. The year after John Bunyan's birth (1629), the second Stuart King, Charles I's experiment of ruling without Parliament began, and two months after Bunyan's death in October 1688, William of Orange came from the Netherlands to save Protestantism in England, and Charles II's second son, James II fled into exile.

'Scholars have difficulty agreeing what exactly caused the English Civil War, which broke out in 1642. Some scholars think the king's personality had a lot to do with it. He had a high-pitched Scots voice with a stammer, and compensated for his insecurity by high-handed actions, for example, ruling without Parliament from 1629-40. He used his control of the judges to enforce his will against his opponents. He turned an ancient law about Ship Money into a means of raising revenue to carry out his policies, and when it was challenged in court, the judges ruled (narrowly) in his favour. Bunyan's county, Bedfordshire, showed widespread opposition to the tax.

'Other scholars saw religion as a key factor, and searched for evidence of a Roman Catholic takeover bid. Charles never supported the Protestant side in the Thirty Years War in Europe, nor did he act to protect or defend Protestant Huguenots in France. In England, Archbishop Laud introduced unwelcome ceremonies into church worship, and a Papal agent was received at Whitehall for the first time for eighty years. Across the border, the Scots were outraged at the imposition of an English Prayer Book on the Scottish churches. The Scottish Parliament recruited a fighting force, and thousands of Scots signed the National Covenant in 1638, many in their own blood, although they retained their own loyalty to the King's person. The English Parliament raised a fighting force which Oliver Cromwell shaped into the New Model Army.

'What did John Bunyan make of all this?' Amy asked.

'It was very difficult for a country lad to make sense of it all. John had problems nearer home, which seemed bigger to him than affairs of State. John Bunyan's mother took ill and died in June 1644. She was buried in Elstow churchyard. He was heartbroken, for he had been very close to his Mum. In July 1644, his sister died. In August 1644, John Bunyan's father remarried. People think John could have been very angry at his father for remarrying so soon after his mother's death, which seemed very thoughtless. This may have been the reason why John went off to join the Parliamentary Army at Newport Pagnell, 13 miles west of Bedford, very soon after his sixteenth birthday. Today the town lies at the north-eastern tip of Milton Keynes. We have no written record of his feelings, but he may well have joined the Army to display his displeasure at his father, take time to grieve for his mother, distance himself from all that was going on at Elstow, and prove his manhood as a soldier.'

'Was joining the Army just a protest and an escape for him?' Amy asked.

'No,' Andy continued: 'Some important things happened to him during his Army service. First of all, he would widen his experience of life. There he would also extend his vocabulary, and learn to swear like a trooper as well as a tinker! His father's influence had already made him a foul-tongued youth—he was no slouch in the swearing stakes! He would also learn from the experience of older men in the Army who had been places and done things beyond the experience of a country bumpkin like John Bunyan. He was posted to the Company of Colonel Richard Cokayne, a Bedfordshire man, in Newport Pagnell. Bedford was one of the seven English counties from which the Parliamentary Army drew its main strength.

'Would John Bunyan join in the questionable talk and activities of these men of the world?' Amy asked.

'Remember, he would be under pressure to fit in. Nobody likes to be isolated or ignored because they do not take part. There are always people who want to take a young man under their wing, so to speak, and lead them into new experiences.'

'What else happened to him? He must have been homesick....Did he pray or turn to God for help?'

'Good point, Amy!' In the Army, he became exposed to Bible and Gospel preaching by fighting men. His fighting and praying Captains became models for his pen-portraits when he came to write 'Pilgrim's Progress'. Some of the Army leaders were men of God, men with a mission to share their experience of God, and their understanding of the Bible with their fellow-soldiers. Wherever possible, Sunday was a day which featured acts of worship, singing, Bible-reading and preaching.

Sometimes these meetings would take place in the open air, and he would also hear sermons in the parish church of Newport Pagnell. John probably had a copy of 'The Soldiers Pocket Bible', which was first issued in 1643. Two of its instructions were 'a soldier must not do wickedly', and 'A soldier must cry unto God in his heart at the very instant of battle'.

'How did the preaching compare with what we hear in our church, Andy? Was it totally different?'

'It would agree with a lot of what our parents call evangelical preaching. We'll talk about theology later, Amy, but there are two things we should remember. First of all, the sermons would be LONGER, Amy! That doesn't necessarily mean they were better! Secondly, the preaching would be based on God's grace rather than our achievement. The modern, scientific age, thinks it has gone a long way since Bunyan's time, and is always wanting to claim credit for its progress, even when a sign of that progress is my commitment to God or the Church. Isn't God lucky to have a clever, gifted person like me as a follower! The preaching of Bunyan's time to any era of history stresses that we are sinners. We may be technological giants, but we're moral pigmies, and the only proper place for us is to be humbled in the dust before a great Saviour, the Lord Jesus Christ. He knows the worst about us and loves us just the same, and wants us to turn from sin to God....'

Andy's voice tailed off, and Amy broke in: 'My, my, is that a pillow I see before me, or a pulpit, Andy Burnett?'

'Sorry, Amy, you got me back on my high horse.'

'He probably formed a special friendship in the Army, with Mathias Cowley, who later published the first literary effort of his Army mate, 'Some Gospel Truths Opened', in 1656. John also formed a lasting friendship with John Gibbs, Puritan minister of St Peter and St Paul's in Newport Pagnell. Gibbs came there in 1647.

'To return to Bunyan the soldier...was he involved in any real fighting?' Amy asked.

'We're not really sure, Amy, but we can have a judicious conjecture, or as the good people of Leahaven say, a guess. He may have fought with Major Ennis on the walls of Leicester against the assault of Prince Rupert's cavalry. He may have taken part in some skirmishing as Captain Bladwell marched to Surrey Downs. Perhaps he listened to Captain Hobson as he preached to the troops mustered in Lathbury Field. The Army began to be disbanded in 1646, and John Bunyan was demobilised in July 1647. He went home to live as a tinker and squirm as a miserable sinner for the next three years.'

'During his time in the Army, something happened which really shook John Bunyan to the core of his being. He was due to take up some military duty, but he was replaced, and the man who replaced him was shot and killed by a musket bullet. From that time on, the question always arose in his mind whether his life had been spared for some great purpose. The spiritual search for God began in earnest in John Bunyan's life....'

There was a brief silence, then Amy said with a naughty grin 'Have we to come back next week for the next thrilling episode? The way you tell them, Andy, it's like listening to a serial with a cliff-hanger at the end of each episode!'

Andy responded in a good-natured way: 'Don't be such a tease, Amy Taylor! Away home to your Mum, and call again soon. Seriously, Amy, you've no idea how investigating John Bunyan has perked me up, and I want to thank you for noticing that I wasn't too well today.'

Amy walked home slowly, reflecting on the tremendous intellectual gifts of Andy the Brain, and feeling grateful for all his time spent on Bunyan for her benefit.

chapter five

FINDING A WIFE AND HEARING A VOICE

'Can I ask you a couple of things about Andy, Mum?' Amy said one Saturday as she was getting ready for her visit. (There were certain advantages to having a trained nurse for a mother.)

'Tell me what it is, Amy, and I'll try to help.'

'He always seems to be coughing and wheezing, Mum.'

'Chronic coughing and wheezing are part of having cystic fibrosis, dear. Anything else?'

'Well, Mum,' Amy proceeded slowly, 'I've noticed that the ends of his fingers are funny—sort of lumpy, and I've noticed this only recently.'

'This is called 'clubbing' Amy, and occurs not only with CF, but also with some of the people born with heart disease and other types of lung problems. It's just another sign that his condition is gradually getting worse.'

Amy was quite tearful on the way to Andy's house that week, but she put on her bravest face to ask Andy about John Bunyan's return home from the Army.

Andy was so pleased to see her, that he breezed on, unaware of her heartache. His dark eyes were full of excitement as he took up his subject again.

'Imagine what it was like, Amy. John Bunyan had survived his military service for about two years and eight months, without any wounds or injuries. He came striding into his home village tall and erect. He was a powerfully built, super-fit nineteen-year-old, with marvellous bronzed skin polished in the open air by the sun, and those flashing blue eyes glinting beneath that shock of reddish-brown hair, and all that adrenalin pumping through his veins. What do you think he would be thinking about, Amy?'

Amy blushed as she answered...'I suppose...a girl friend... love...and marriage,' she replied, her girlish intuition showing.

'Got it in one, Amy!' Andy chuckled. 'We know where they lived, but we don't even know the bride's name.

The penniless pair moved into a cottage in Elstow. Although the property known as 'Bunyan's Cottage' was demolished in 1968, we can still see white, half-timbered cottages with overhanging their storey, of a similar type, today.

The scant mention his family receives in John Bunyan's writings is incredible, but it is a fair deduction to think that his wife was called Mary. They got married in 1649, and since their first child, born blind, was called Mary, you don't have to be a rocket scientist to guess that his wife was named Mary too. Since blind Mary was baptized on 20 July 1650, we may guess that they were married not later than October 1649, a month before John's twenty-first birthday. Mrs. John Bunyan was probably not a local girl. Perhaps he met her when he was in the Army, or on his travels as a tinker.'

'What about John and his father? Was the possible problem in that relationship sorted out?' Amy asked.

'We don't have any direct evidence, but it may be an indication of the strain between them that the first child of his Dad's second marriage was named Charles. Charles, after all, was the king John and the Parliamentary Army were fighting against.'

'Did John ever write a description of his wife?' Amy asked.

'He said two things about her. First, she had a godly father: 'my mercy was to light upon a wife whose father was counted godly.'

Second, John Bunyan and his wife began their married life as poor as church mice. Bunyan wrote: 'This woman and I...came together as poor as poor might be, not having so much household stuff as a dish or a spoon betwixt us both.' His wife's only material contribution to the marriage were two small and simple books called 'The Plain Man's Pathway to Heaven', and 'The Practice of Piety', which her father had left her when he died.' His wife often read extracts from these to her wild young husband.

'Have you any idea how they got on together?' Amy asked.

'Mrs. Bunyan was a well-trained and tactful Christian girl. She often spoke to John about her father's godly character, and in her duties at home she brought Christian influences to bear on her young husband, without ramming Christianity down his throat. She tried to embody the approach set out for wives with non-Christian husbands in 1 Peter 3 verses 1-4: 'Wives, in the same way be submissive to your husbands so that, if any of them do not believe the word, they may be won over without words by the behaviour of their wives, when they see the purity and reverence of your lives. Your beauty should not come from outward adornment, such as braided hair and the wearing of gold jewellery and fine clothes. Instead, it should be that of your inner self, the unfading beauty of a gentle and quiet spirit, which is of great worth in God's sight.'

'Their love and affection for each other comforted John for the first time since his mother's death. His wife steered a wise course between seeming indifference about his wrongdoing, and constantly moaning about his behaviour.'

'What was wrong about his behaviour?' Amy asked.

'Well, it was true that they read these books together, and because of his wife's influence, Bunyan attended church regularly, but if we believe what he writes about himself, he sang like a saint on a Sunday, and sinned like a devil (he wrote 'I retained my wicked life') for the rest of the week.'

'His heart was a whirlpool of seething religious emotion, superstition and fear, just like the society in which he lived.'

'What was he afraid of?' Amy asked.

'He was possibly haunted by his past. In his book 'Grace Abounding', he says 'until I came to the state of marriage, I was the very ringleader of all the youths that kept me company in all manner of vices and ungodliness.' He was probably also scared of the judgement of God for his bad language. He came back from the Army he says as 'a brisk talker' and 'a great sin-breeder.' In his own words, he said he 'infected all the youth of the town where I was born with all manner of youthful vanities.' He was probably also worried about guilt-by-association with his best friend, 'who was a wicked creature for cursing, swearing and whoring (chasing after vile women).' Bunyan admits to being a great swearer himself, although he claims to have been sexually pure after his marriage.'

'They say a man is known by the company he keeps,' Amy chimed in...but perhaps John Bunyan exaggerated his wickedness in a well-meaning attempt to make God's kindness seem greater.'

'That's a possibility, Amy' said Andy, 'but his fight against many demons, real or imaginary, reflects the belief-systems of the world and the times he lived in.'

'What kind of beliefs are you talking about?' Amy asked.

'Let's leave that minefield for your next visit,' Andy explained. 'Let me tell you about the voice he heard. He had been to church, and the vicar, Christopher Hall, launched a verbal attack on those who took part in Sunday sport on the village green. The best plan is to listen to what John Bunyan said about it...'In the midst of a game at cat...just as I was about to strike it the second time, a voice did suddenly dart from heaven into my heart.' The voice said 'wilt thou leave thy sins and go to heaven, or have thy sins and go to hell?'

The Voice on the Village Green drove Bunyan into a private wrestling match with all that was evil. He argued that it was miserable to sin, and yet miserable not to sin. He said that

Satan suggested that it was just as well to be condemned for many sins as for a few. Bunyan's spiritual roller-coaster was like the story of the Red Indian chief.'

'What was that all about,' said Amy with a puzzled look.

'He said it was as if there were two dogs inside him, fighting to take over his life, a black dog and a white dog. When he was asked which one was winning, he said it was the one he fed the most....

'Come back next week, Amy, and get ready for a theology lesson!'

chapter six

PICK-AND-MIX RELIGION

When Amy arrived on the following Saturday, Andy offered her an escape from the maze of ideas he was about to present.

'I realise that this will be very confusing for a simple soul,' he said,' because I know the bother I had trying to sort it all out, and learning to express it simply. I keep remembering that slogan 'K-I-S-S' (keep it simple stupid!), and I would understand anyone who wanted to skip this chapter. It's probably worth sticking at it and gaining some understanding of the world of odd ideas Bunyan faced. Remember the final instruction in the old Scots golf manual: 'Finally, never give up—your opponent might die!'

'There were all sorts of groups, large and small, in Bunyan's time, with odd names and titles for each group. Sometimes the name was really a nickname, so it is useful for marking out the distinctive features of each group, and giving a clue about what they believed.

'The main church body was of course the Church of England, which had gone through the Protestant Reformation. The Pope's authority was no longer valid, and the monarch was Supreme Governor of the Church of England. The English Reformation was imposed from above, started by King Henry VIII, in contrast with the Scottish Reformation which was a grass-roots movement driven by the ordinary people. There was a large and vocal minority within this Anglican Church, or the Church of England, which thought that the Reformation had not gone far enough. They wanted to get rid of the 'bells and smells', images, crucifixes, candles, fancy robes, and those trappings of worship which reminded them of Roman Catholicism. They had strong sympathies with the Reformed faith as it was known in Switzerland and France. They wanted a simpler, PURER kind of worship, so they were called the PURITANS. John Bunyan was mainly Puritan in his beliefs.

John Bunyan was connected briefly to the RANTERS, who RANTED about their personal experience of God, and denied the authority of the Bible. The DIGGERS got their cruel nickname from opponents because they reckoned their leaders were inferior clergy, and were only fit for DIGGING graves. The LEVELLERS were strongly political, agitating for a LEVEL or democratic society where there was no monarchy, and absolute freedom of religion. The DIPPERS or BAPTISTS believed in total immersion in water of those who had reached an age of understanding and faith in God. The QUAKERS were so named because their followers sometimes QUAKED or trembled at their religious meetings. The INDEPENDENTS were in favour of church order which was free from State control or interference. The CONGREGATIONALISTS argued for the freedom of individual CONGREGATIONS to rule their affairs under God. The LATITUDINARIANS believed in giving LATITUDE, or freedom, to a wide range of views on Christian belief, organisation and church practice. The FIFTH MONARCHY MEN aimed at bringing in the FIFTH MONARCHY after the four Empires in the Bible Book of Daniel—Assyria, Persia, Greece and Rome—and many of them believed Oliver Cromwell's Commonwealth would lead to the establishment of the Fifth Monarchy. The MILLENARIANS believed that Jesus Christ would return to earth and reign for a MILLENIUM, that is, a thousand years. This was an accepted ancient belief which was taken up by many Independents in Bunyan's period. Bunyan shared their belief, and it shows in his writings. In his early writings, John Bunyan wrote against the Ranters and the Quakers. The Bedford Church which Bunyan joined eventually was an Independent church with Congregational and Baptist leanings, following a Puritan theology! They loved the Puritans' very strong appeal to the Bible as the only source book for Christian life and church order.

'Is that enough, Amy?

'My brain is bursting, Andy', Amy retorted, and quoted from the poem 'The Deserted Village'

'And still they gazed, and still their wonder grew,
That one small head could carry all he knew.'

'That's not all, Amy. The two leaders of the Protestant

Reformation in Europe were an Augustinian monk named Martin Luther, who was German, and a French lawyer named John Calvin, who tried to set up a model Christian State in Geneva, Switzerland. Luther, formerly a Roman Catholic monk and academic, defied the might of the Roman Catholic Church in order to spread his teaching about being right with God through faith rather than religious duties. Luther's translation of the Bible into bold, powerful German was a major factor in the formation of a united Germany. Many of the Christians of the time followed CALVINISTIC teaching, which came from JOHN CALVIN, who had a brain like a razor, and was able to set out brilliant summaries of Christian belief based on the Bible. They fitted their Christian beliefs into a framework which came from Calvin's booklet—'The Institutes of the Christian Religion'—whose teaching was cleverly summarised by John Owen with the acrostic word T-U-L-I-P.

T=Total Depravity. We are not all totally bad, but there is no part of our nature unaffected by sin.

U=Unconditional Election. God chooses His elect, not everyone, for salvation, and by implication chooses the majority for damnation and hell.

L=Limited Atonement. Jesus died only for the elect, so that the 'all' and 'whosoever' references in the Bible mean 'all without distinction' rather than 'all without exception'.

I=Irresistible Grace. God's kindness in salvation means that His grace draws the elect to Him in such a way that they cannot resist.

P=Perseverance of the Saints. The faith of the elect

believers will persist so that they will ultimately go to heaven. The elect cannot be 'saved' and later 'lost'.

'Good grief!' said Amy. 'How did John Bunyan make sense of all that!'

'With difficulty!' Andy replied. He had initial contact with the Ranters. He wrote against the Quakers, but contact with persecuted Quakers in prison softened his views on them. It is amusing that in the present day both Baptists and Congregationalists claim Bunyan as one of theirs. His theology certainly had the same Calvinist emphasis as that of the Puritans.

'Back to the young John Bunyan', Andy resumed. 'He lived in a world of superstition, populated with demons, who were the servants of that old Serpent, the Devil, or Satan, dedicated to his downfall.' John Bunyan described his past misery in his book published in 1666, 'Grace Abounding to the Chief of Sinners'. 'Grace Abounding' is a fascinating story of a man's search for and discovery of God, but there are bits missed out that leave us with huge questions about John Bunyan. We can neither work out the timescale nor explain why he hardly mentions his children, his first wife's death or his remarriage. We do get a clear picture of someone facing the agonies of temptation and despair. He was haunted by the grotesque carvings in wood and stone in the church.

'As I said earlier, even the church bells had religious overtones! He loved bell-ringing, but gave it up (he was Number 4 in the mathematical change of peals.) He even gave up watching the bell-ringers, in case the bells should fall from the roof and land on his head. He later kept a respectful distance from the bell-tower, scared that it would collapse on top of him as an act of God's judgement.

'Did any of the people in the village notice changes in Bunyan's life?' Amy asked.

'They must have,' Andy replied. 'As well as giving up bell-ringing, John Bunyan also stopped swearing, which would have surprised a local woman shopkeeper, who rebuked him for swearing, and made him wish, he said, 'with all my heart that I might be a little child again, that my father might learn me to speak without this wicked way of swearing.'

'He was locked in a life-or-death struggle between his wife's goodness and the vicar's preaching on the one hand, and his old habits on the other. He loved dancing, but after a year of private torture, he gave up joining the revellers in the Moot Hall on the village green. The Moot Hall was probably built in the sixteenth century, and has been refurbished in its old style. It is a curious red brick and timber building, with a projecting upper storey.

'Is this kind of personal torture just part of the period when he lived, or is it something more widespread?' Amy asked.

Andy responded immediately. 'Good point, Amy. There was a lot of gloom and misery about in the middle decades of the seventeenth century. That is why Doubting Castle and Giant Despair would be very real to the readers of 'Pilgrim's Progress.' Some scholars have gathered evidence of well-known people of the period who committed suicide, and there is widespread evidence of children taking their own lives. The people at the bottom of the heap, as well as a few well-known ones at the top, felt trapped, and unable to cope with personal circumstances or national events.

'Did the monarchy contribute to this despair which the people felt?' Amy asked.

'Sure thing,' said Andy. The Stuart Kings believed in the Divine Right of Kings with respect to the monarchy, and the Divine Right of Episcopacy (church rule by bishops) with respect to the church.

James VI of Scotland who was also James I of England had a slogan 'no bishop, no king!' He said that 'presbytery agrees as well with monarchy, as God and the devil!' There was great political upheaval, with Parliament killing King Charles I, Cromwell refusing offers to become King, the Restoration of constitutional monarchy under King Charles II in 1660, and so on. This all bred uncertainty. The great economic changes, especially in ownership and management of land, made the lucky few richer, and the poor got poorer. The teaching about predestination was a strengthening doctrine for some, and plunged others into despair, and even suicide. Religious conversion was one possible answer. Many Christians down through the years have had distinctive experiences of conversion. Back in the sixteenth century, the great Reformer Martin Luther had wrestled with God until he found peace and faith. Bunyan's future pastor, John Gifford, was converted to Christ around 1650.

'Bunyan, like many others, won through to a tough faith. The spiritual autobiography (testimony story) became a literary type from about 1650. For the first time, people could read about despair and deliverance. Of course, John Bunyan would identify himself with the apostle Paul's description of himself in the Bible: 'I do not understand what I do. For what I want to do I do not do, but what I hate, I do....I agree that the law is good. As it is, it is no longer I myself who do it, but it is sin living in me... what a wretched man I am! Who will rescue me from this body of death?' (Romans 7 v 15,16,24.) Bunyan was so disturbed in his spirit and struggle that he thought for a while that his baby Mary was born blind as a punishment from God for his sins!

'What is religious conversion?' Amy asked.

'We hear this often at our church, Amy. Conversion means turning—conversion is a turning to Christ and a change of life, Amy. It's a new life rather than a new lifestyle. It's a turning from self-sufficiency to Christ-sufficiency. It's a turning from trusting in my goodness to trusting in God's kindness. It's a change of direction in life, where you turn from sin and going your own way, to turn to God and going His way. You throw yourself on the mercy and forgiveness which flows from all that Jesus has done for us, by giving His body, and shedding His blood on the Cross.'

'Many thanks, O Great One! Can I ask you a personal question, Andy? Nothing to do with conversion?'

'Fire away' said Andy.

'How did they find out at the start that you had cystic fibrosis?'

'They do a sweat test, which analyses the amount of sodium and chloride in a person's sweat. They apply an odourless, colourless, sweat-producing chemical to a small area on your arms or legs. An electrode is attached to the area, which stimulates a weak electric current, causing a warm, tingling feeling. The sweat collected was sent to a laboratory for analysis. They repeated the sweat test, and did a genetic analysis of a blood sample to confirm that it was CF.'

'Thank you, Andy the Super-Brain, Answerer of all my questions. Medical Science sounds even more complicated than theology. See you next Saturday, I hope!'

chapter seven

NEW PREACHER, NEW LIFE

Amy positively rushed into Andy's room the following Saturday, took off her anorak as quickly as possible, and started questioning Andy.

'C'mon Andy, put us out of our misery! How did John Bunyan get out of his misery?' she asked.

'You'll remember we talked about how he seemed a reformed character, yet his heart was like a volcano? Well, the way to deliverance came when he was working normally in the streets of Bedford. He overheard three women sitting in a doorway, enjoying the sunshine, and talking naturally about the things of God.'

'What do you mean by 'the things of God', asked Amy.

They were talking about how God had worked in their hearts to give them what they called 'the new birth'. John Bunyan was a good talker, yet he was out of his depth here.... But he couldn't help noticing how pleasant, natural, and joyful their conversation was. They spoke as if they had discovered a new world, and he was out of it.'

'How did this affect him?'

'He didn't feel threatened by these ordinary ladies, and he opened up his heart to them, and became more desperate than ever to know God intimately and personally. Poor John! He ransacked the Bible for help, and cried out to God in prayer. The ladies mentioned his need to John Gifford, who had become the pastor of their Bedford congregation in 1650. Bunyan talked things over with the godly Gifford, and soon joined his congregation. Texts from the Bible were flying across Bunyan's mind, like balls in a tennis tournament, as he searched for salvation and peace.

'What effect had this on his wife?' Amy asked anxiously.

'She watched John like a spectator, and prayed for him, and spurred him on in his search for Jesus. John got the opportunity to read Martin Luther's 'Commentary on the Epistle to the Galatians', which he loved. He said it was 'most fit for a wounded conscience.' His inner struggle lasted for just over a year.

Amy continued: 'How important was John Gifford in this spiritual search?'

'He was vital, Amy. John Gifford had been a Royalist officer during the Civil War. He had been a notorious blasphemer, drunkard and gambler. Through the help of his sister, Gifford had escaped from Maidstone Jail the night before his execution. (She came to visit him, and found the guards were drunk and asleep!) He eventually married and started a new life in Bedford as a doctor. After a particularly heavy loss at gambling, and a fit of drunken temper, Gifford had a remarkable religious conversion as a result of reading a Puritan book by Thomas Bolton. After his own conversion he became a wise and holy man of God. The members of his congregation had separated from the Church of England, followed Puritan doctrine, and practised the baptism of believers by total immersion in water. Gifford encouraged love, unity and social equality among his people. He called for the richer members of the congregation to give more generously so that 'the necessities of those who are in want' could be met by the Lord's people.

'How did John Bunyan fit into this group? Did being a tinker hold him back?' Amy asked.

'Not a bit! He fitted in very well. They accepted him in 1653. He was baptized and became a full member in 1655, shortly before John Gifford's death. He was probably baptized, at night, in a little inlet of the River Ouse at Duck Mill, Bedford.

Bunyan accepted and agreed with Gifford's view that baptism was not a necessary condition for admission to the church, as long as the candidates gave a satisfactory account of their faith. Their views on baptism affected Bunyan, because he took advantage of the recently-introduced civil registration of births to have his second daughter, Elizabeth, registered as 'born in April 1654,' not baptized in the parish church. Soon after her birth, probably in 1655, the Bunyan family left Elstow, and went to live in Bedford, in the parish of St Cuthberts, North of the River Ouse, in a house with two living-rooms on either side of the front door, and a single gable window above. Their third and fourth children, both boys (John and Thomas) born before 1658, do not even seem to have been registered.'

Andy asked Amy for what he called 'a private moment', for which he apologised. Amy offered to go home, but Andy's Dad steered Amy downstairs for her usual drink and biscuit, which was usually brought up to them.

'I'm sorry, Amy,' Andy's Dad explained. 'Cystic fibrosis makes sufferers prone to chronic diarrhoea, and Andy's been having a bad week. It's just one of those things. He shrugged his shoulders. 'I'm sure Andy will want you to be there as soon as he's comfortable again. His Mum will attend to him. Many thanks for taking time to visit him.'

Within 15 minutes, Amy was back in the room.

'Now, where was I?' Andy asked. 'Oh, yes, we had John Bunyan well and truly committed as a member of the Bedford congregation. In 1655, three very important things shook John Bunyan to the foundation of his being—three things affecting his family, his minister, and his life.'

'Now, take it easy, Andy,' Amy said gently. She had noticed that he had suddenly tired. 'Tell me briefly what they were, and we'll finish up for today.'

Andy resumed his story:

'First, John Bunyan's wife died. He lost the one who had shared in all his trials, and he was left to look after four little children, the eldest only seven years old, and she was blind.'

'Second, his pastor, John Gifford died. His last words to his congregation were to plead with them to walk in love, as

Christ had loved them. He was succeeded by John Burton, a young Baptist in failing health, who had enormous respect for his tinker member. John Burton died in September 1660.'

'Third, around the time of John Gifford's death, some of the ablest members of the church urged Bunyan to speak a word of encouragement from the Bible at one of their small gatherings. His great gifts as a preacher were immediately recognised and confirmed by his fellow-members. As he spoke further afield, more and more people travelled to hear what the tinker had to say, and his words deeply affected his hearers. Within a short time, he was set apart as a preacher by his own congregation, and new areas of service were opened up for him, first as a preacher and then as a writer. Around the time of John Burton's death, the independent congregation lost its building, and had to meet mainly in farm buildings, kindly loaned.'

'Can I ask a favour, Amy?' Andy said.

'Of course, my good friend—your wish is my command!'

Andy laughed. 'I've run out of material....Could you leave it for at least two weeks before you come back?'

Amy readily agreed, and headed for home.

chapter eight

BRAVING THE STORM

Three weeks later, Amy breezed into a room bathed in Leahaven sunshine, and said 'Have you done your homework, Andy? Where do you get your facts? What are we going to talk about today?'

'One at a time's good fishing, Amy. But to take them in order, the answer to Question one is 'yes', the answer to Question two I am not telling you, but in these days there are internet sites as well as over 800 books, and in answer to Question three, I think we should talk about English society and its class divisions in Bunyan's time. That seems a hard task, but it will help us to understand what a bunch of dolly mixtures John Bunyan had in his congregation, and how he came to be in prison for over twelve years. An academic (Christopher Hill) wrote a book about John Bunyan and his church, and the title is 'A Turbulent, Seditious, and Factious People'.

'Jumpin' stuff, Andy! I didn't realise we were studying such a long-term prisoner....'

'Christians have a long pedigree in the jail sentence department, Amy. It must have been very difficult for such a man of action to be hemmed in for so long.'

Amy looked thoughtful. 'I've always thought that preachers were very respectable people, Andy.'

The apostle Paul saw the inside of a few prisons in his time. When you look at Bunyan's congregation, you discover there were some very respectable people, and perhaps a few 'hooks, crooks and comic singers' as well! Some scholars think that Bunyan himself may have been a political extremist.'

'How did that happen?' Amy asked innocently.

'The seventeenth century, more than any before, brought a huge division between the rich and the poor. At the rich end of the scale, enormous wealth poured into the coffers of the rich after the Protestant Reformation meant that the wealth and land formerly owned by the Roman Catholic Church was 'up for grabs'. By the seventeenth century, those who benefited were enjoying the spoils of their pickings. The New World had brought new markets within reach of wealthy merchants, and these markets expanded in tune with a world population explosion. Pushy merchants and dealers expanded their wealth and exploited their advantages by gobbling up the assets of the poor. Some families, like the Bunyans, had to gradually sell off parcels of land, and saw their independence vanishing like the Cheshire cat in Alice in Wonderland, except that there was no grin left either....

'At the bottom of the heap was a growing gang of discontented people, landless labourers and angry vagabonds, whose labour and lives became the trading pieces in a kind of English slavery. Education has always been a ladder of escape for the poor, but these hard times meant that little children had to work to keep families alive. There was little time or money for schooling. A major change in farming methods acted like the tightening jaws of a vice closing in on the poor. Before this time, fields were divided into strips, each cultivated by a family within a community. The movement to enclose fields gave the rich a 'double whammy' over the poor. First, only those with enough money could afford to hedge or fence off their fields. Second, the enclosure movement denied the poor the ground on which to grow their food. They had to sell their labour to the rich to get money to buy food, and this increased their poverty and misery. They felt trapped. No wonder hundreds braved the Atlantic Ocean to take their chance and make a new life in the New World.'

'You seem to be very severe on the rich, Andy,' said Amy. 'Are there things you're not telling me? Did they exploit their positions in other ways.'

'In the majority of cases, the poor received no mercy. The gentry not only owned the land, they controlled the justice system locally, so that poor people had virtually no rights. Many rural properties were owned by the landlord, so any refusal to work for the landlord made a family homeless. Local courts imposed fines and increased taxes, so that the poor became helpless slaves. Where any crime was suspected, the houses of the poor were searched first. Oliver Goldsmith, a poet from the next century, summed it up well:

> *Ill fares the land, to hastening ills a prey,*
> *Where wealth accumulates, and men decay...*

'Did any church or Christian leaders speak out against all this?' Amy asked indignantly.

'Some debated whether it was permissible to steal to keep your family alive, but others, like the godly Richard Baxter, argued that it was a poor man's Christian duty to watch his family die quietly. Labourers and paupers formed about half the population.

'That's outrageous! Where did John Bunyan's congregation fit in?' Amy asked.

'That's a very good question, Amy. First of all, we have to recognise that Bunyan functioned for about five years as a preacher while working as a tinker. In the New Testament, we read that the apostle Paul combined preaching and tent-making. John Bunyan had no formal training to be a preacher. Hundreds of people came to hear John Bunyan, who travelled widely to preach the Good News about Jesus. He often went on horseback, around Bedfordshire, Hertford, Buckingham and Huntingdon.

Sometimes he preached in barns, or wooded areas, or beside sheltered river banks, or in private homes. The congregation saw the difficulties he was facing, and gave him tremendous prayer and practical support. In 1658, he was indicted at Assizes for preaching at Eaton. In May 1659, he was preaching in Mr. Ainger's barn on a farm near Toft, five miles west of Cambridge, when he was challenged by the Reverend Professor Dr Thomas Smith. The professor denied the right of a layman to preach, or of the Bedford Church to send him to preach. Someone wrote to Professor Smith later, saying: 'You seem to be angry with the tinker because he strives to mend souls as well as pots and pans.'

'When John Bunyan became aware of the increasing hostility of the Established Church and the Law's representatives, he recognised that his days of freedom could be numbered, and that he had to take steps to provide care for his children. The godly Elizabeth agreed to become his wife, and mother to his children. She proved to be a loyal and loving wife and stepmother from the time of their marriage in 1659.

'The founders of the Bedford Church included two men who had been mayors of the town of Bedford, and another two were officials in Oliver Cromwell's State Church. Richard Cooper, mayor of Bedford in 1657, was also a member of the church, and one member also sat as a member in the Barebones Parliament.'

'That's a funny name for a Parliament!' Amy interrupted. 'How did that come about?'

'The leading figure in that Parliament was Praise-God Barebones, and before you say that is a funny Christian name, another leader in the same Parliament was 'Look-Unto-Me-And-Be-Ye-Saved Smith!' Andy replied.

'What kind of jobs did the Bedford members have?' Amy asked.

'As well as the leading figures mentioned above, there were people of the 'butcher and baker and candlestick maker' variety—shopkeepers, hatters, heelmakers, cobblers and of course a famous brazier or tinker.'

'Back to the main plot!' Andy continued, 'by 1659 the congregation was described as 'Baptists' or 'Anabaptists' ('re-baptizers'), and although the church supported John, the gentry in the area seemed to mark him out as a possible trouble-maker and rabble-rouser, and they tried to bring pressure on him to give up preaching, and return to be a tinker full-time.'

'Why didn't he do that, and save his wife and family, and his church a lot of grief and heartache?'

'That seems a sensible solution at first glance, Amy, but there are several reasons why he wouldn't.

First of all, he loved preaching, and felt called and gifted to do it. The Arabs say that the best speaker is someone 'who can turn the ear into an eye.' John Bunyan had the rare gift of making Bible truth visual and pictorial, so that hearers could see and grasp the truths he was teaching.

Second, the call of God to John had been confirmed by the Bedford Church setting him apart, and by many ordinary people responding to his preaching by giving themselves to God. He said 'I preached what I did feel, what I smartingly did feel.' John Gibbs, minister at Newport Pagnell, wrote in a preface to one of John Bunyan's books: 'God hath counted him faithful, and put him into the ministry; and though his outward condition and former employment was mean, and his human learning small, yet is he one that hath acquaintance with God...and hath been used in His hand to do souls good.' John was a big young man with a powerful voice, and his inner conviction got through to his hearers. We'll recognise a lot more of his pictorial gifts when we come to talk about his famous book 'Pilgrim's Progress'.... Andy's voice trailed away in tiredness.

'Oh, go on, Andy, give us a for-instance,' Amy spurred him on.

'Alright,' said Andy 'Here's a for-instance. In Pilgrim's Progress, Pilgrim reaches the Interpreter's House, and he sees a painting which sums up Bunyan's view of a preacher. Some think it was a description of John Gifford. Others think it could even be a self-portrait. The picture was of 'a very serious person. He had eyes lifted up to heaven, the best of books in his hand, the law of truth was written on his lips, the world was behind his back. He stood as if he pleaded with men, and a crown of gold did hang over his head.' Bunyan was more like a prophet than a priest. A priest speaks to God on behalf of people. A prophet speaks to people on behalf of God.

'Here's another for-instance from John Bunyan: 'I saw through grace that it was the blood shed on Mount Calvary that did save and redeem sinners, as clearly and as really with the eyes of my soul as ever methought I had seen a penny loaf bought with a penny.'

'So John Gifford had gone, and John Burton had gone. Before his death, John Burton gave his verdict on John Bunyan : this man is not chosen out of an earthly, but out of the heavenly university.' John Burton had solid support from the Bedford Church, but they knew that he was a fearless risk-taker. By 1659 he had written against the Ranters and the Quakers, and had met opposition from the Law and the Established Church. He had also faced the kind of criticism which is directed against Christian preachers. They said he had two wives and accused him of behaving immorally. One particular piece of gossip centred on Agnes Beaumont, a girl who joined the Bunyan meeting church at Gamlingay, near the Cambridgeshire border. Her widowed father had stopped going to church and became an opponent of Bunyan. She had organised a lift on horseback from John Wilson, a pastor from Hitchin, who would take her the seven miles to the meeting.

It was the dead of winter and walking was out of the question. He failed to appear, and her brother's horse was not available. Unexpectedly, Bunyan rode by on his way to the same meeting, and eventually agreed to the pleadings of Agnes' brother, and took her there. When she got home, her father had locked her out and the rumour factory started! John Bunyan's response was, as usual, straightforward. He said that if all the impure men in England were hanged by the neck till they were dead, John Bunyan would still be alive and well!

In 1660, a series of events which hit him like thunderclaps made a drastic change in his life. The hounds of opposition and persecution which were like puppies when he started off as a preacher, became full-grown, and were barking at his heels. In 1660, they caught up with him.'

'Come back next week, Amy, and by that time I'll tell you all about it.' Andy fell back on his pillow, his eyes closed. He gave a weak wave, and Amy slipped quietly out of the room.

chapter nine

THE TRAP CLOSES

The following Saturday was as wet a day as Amy could remember. The drains could hardly cope with the volume of rainwater.

Amy usually walked across town to Andy's house, just for the exercise, but this time she had to ask her Mum to take her in the car.

'Hail, Oh Wet One!' Andy greeted her when she came into the room. 'Is it true that fishermen fish under bridges on days like this?

'Why would they do that?' Amy looked puzzled.

'Well the fish go there to keep out of the rain....' Andy managed a broad grin. 'I'll tell you one good thing about a day like this, Amy. It's a good thing our skin is waterproof, or we'd all be in a soggy mess!'

'I can see we're in for trouble today, Andy, with you in this bouncy sort of mood.'

'I'm sorry, Amy, but John Bunyan's plight reminded me of an essay I once read about dangerous occupations. The pupil had chosen an airline pilot's job as a dangerous occupation, and she gave a series of paragraphs on what could happen—engine failure, passengers taking heart attacks, football hooligans making a disturbance, hijackers, and so on. Every paragraph finished with the same words: 'And there was the poor airline pilot in trouble again.'

'We saw last time how trouble was building up for John Bunyan. To understand better what happened to him, we have to see 'the big picture' in the events which followed the Restoration of King Charles II. I feel I have to warn you, Amy, you're not going to like this. This is the darkest part of the story. Charles II and his Parliament are going to make you angry, Amy!'

'Oh, stop piling on the agony, and get on with it! How did he come back?'

'Parliament decided to restore the monarchy, and Charles II was proclaimed king on 8 May and returned to London on 29 May. On 14 April 1660, Charles II issued from Breda a Declaration of 'liberty to tender consciences, that no man shall be disquieted or called into question for differences of opinion in matters of religion which do not disturb the peace of the kingdom.'

Nothing could be further from the truth. His first Parliament was fiercely royalist and Anglican, and with their support Charles swung into action like a flying anvil.

'Charles II was an unscrupulous, immoral liar with a three-point agenda in his clever mind. Point One was 'not to go on my travels again', that is, he hoped to preserve his own position and avoided being beheaded or exiled. Point Two was at the opportune time to declare himself openly as a Roman Catholic, and restore Roman Catholicism as Britain's State Religion. Point Three was to establish absolutist government in Britain. He had already been declared king in Scotland, and pretended to support the Solemn League and Covenant, to win them over. The Scots had far more in common with Cromwell and the English Puritans than with the Stuart kings. It is one of the sad chapters of Scottish history that their loyalty to an unworthy dynasty led them to fight and die for an unprincipled rogue like Charles II. If you plugged him into a lie detector, Amy, he would fuse the National Grid!

'He already had Scottish support. Now he enlisted the help of Louis XIV, king of France. He made a secret treaty with him when the time was ripe to declare himself openly as a Roman Catholic, and with Louis' help put Points Two and Three of his 'agenda' into action.'

'How did he attack religion?' Amy asked.

'After he secured his political base, he set about any religious opponents like a butcher attacks a carcase with a cleaver...He acted to cut off all Puritans from the Church of England, to turn all those who would not conform to his laws into Dissenters, and then to cut off all Dissenters from holding any local or central position of authority.

'Stage One was to organise a gathering of Anglican church leaders in Convocation at Canterbury and York. In 1661 they made six hundred alterations to the Book of Common Prayer (the Church of England's rule book for church worship), none of which met Puritan desires or demands. None of these alterations were debated in the House of Commons or the House of Lords. The Revised Book of Common Prayer was simply attached to a Bill in July 1661, which received the royal assent on 19 May 1662 as the Act of Uniformity. The only valid service for worship in Anglican churches was that laid down in the Revised Book of Common Prayer. Anyone using another service would suffer heavy penalties. Each clergyman was required by 24 August 1662 (St Bartholomew's Day) to make a personal and official oath of 'unfeigned assent and consent to all and everything prescribed therein.'

'That's ridiculous!' Amy erupted. 'Where's the freedom there?'

'Well, Amy, we are used to making our own choices about religion, but this was a different scene,' said Andy. 'The practical outcome was that about 2000 ministers were ejected from their churches (and vicarages).

Amy was outraged. 'How could they get away with that! Imagine the hardship that would bring on 2000 families!'

'Amy, remember that King and Parliament are a powerful team, Andy said with a quiet intensity.

'Stage Two was to damp down any attempts at written protest. The Act of 1661 against 'tumultuous petitioning' forbade the collection of more than twenty signatures to any petition to King or Parliament which had not been approved by three or more justices of the peace.

'Was that the end of the bad news?' asked Amy.

'You are jesting. Having driven so many Anglicans out,

Charles now acted to make sure neither they nor anyone else was going to organise gatherings for worship. The Conventicle Act of 1664 banned meetings for worship in private houses or elsewhere, where more than five people met (in addition to the family), if their worship was anything other than what was prescribed in the Revised Book of Common Prayer.

'We used to read and hear about the Underground Church in Communist dictatorships. Does that mean we had an Underground Church here in England?'

Correct. There were other pressures brought to bear on the poor, on what are called 'customary rights' like wood-gathering, turf-cutting, and other means by which poor people kept alive. New and severe laws protected game, with savage penalties for breaking them. Many people lived on farm cottages. If they displeased their landlords they could be turned out of their homes, or have their rents increased.

'Stage Three was the final part of the 'thunderclap' I referred to last week—the Five Mile Act of 1665. Any person in Holy Orders, or 'pretended Holy Orders' who had preached at a conventicle and had not taken the oath condemning armed resistance to the king and pledging no attempt at 'any alteration of government either in church or State', was forbidden to live within five miles of any incorporated town or city, or within the same distance of the former place of his ministry. This of course excluded any Dissenters from any share in local or central government. The Five Mile Act hit Dissenters hardest because their congregations were chiefly situated in the towns.'

Amy broke her stunned silence: 'I suppose all this had an impact on John Bunyan.'

Andy continued: 'The gentry already had him on their hit list as a potential trouble-maker. They regarded the person they called 'the tinker' as an imposter and ridiculed his claims to have any authority to preach as a piece of colossal cheek. After 1660, it was abundantly clear how the political and religious wind was blowing. The only safe course of action was to be pro-monarchy, pro-Revised Book of Common Prayer, and as strongly anti-Dissenter as you could be.'

'John Bunyan's position was also clear. He was the vigorous and outspoken opponent of the Revised Book of Common Prayer being forced on congregations. He would have agreed with the Scot Samuel Rutherford, who said 'it is against the nature of prayer for it to be written.' Bunyan was nobody's fool. He knew that although the laws were stacking up against him, it was difficult to enforce them locally. He could have continued to preach for sometime by travelling outside the boundaries of hard-line officials, and by continuing to meet secretly.'

'Why didn't he do that, and keep himself free, his family fed, and his congregations encouraged by his preaching?' Amy asked.

Andy thought for a minute. 'I think there were three reasons, Amy. He felt as a Christian citizen of England, he had done nothing wrong. Secondly, he felt he should take a stand against the evil powers closing in on him. Thirdly, he was a great believer in the providence of God, and that he could trust God to take care of him, and his family, and his congregation.'

'Come on, Andy, put me out of my misery! You've got me on the edge of my chair! How did things work out?'

'On 12 November 1660, he was travelling thirteen miles from Bedford to take a service at Lower Samsell, near Harlington. He heard from his congregation that if he tried to preach, a local magistrate, Francis Wingate, was going to have him arrested. Bunyan had about an hour before the constable would appear. If he left before the constable came, nothing would happen. They tried to persuade John Bunyan to call off his preaching, but he thought carefully, then began to speak, and the constable appeared with a warrant for his arrest. When they arrived at Wingate's house, he had gone out, and Bunyan was released when a friend promised he would appear in the morning.'

'The following morning, Bunyan was taken to Harlington Manor, and to an oak-panelled room where the magistrate Francis Wingate questioned Bunyan and the constable about the meeting that had taken place, and tried to find whether any of the people were armed. The constable insisted there were only a few people present, and there was no sign of trouble. Wingate tried to provoke John Bunyan by swearing to break the neck of all such meetings, but Bunyan gave a soft answer that 'it may be so'. Wingate refused to allow bail unless Bunyan promised to give up preaching, but John said he would not be silent for the sake of freedom. The last Quarter Sessions a month before had merely provided for the restoration of the Prayer Book in church worship. The Act of Uniformity lay ahead in the future. As Justice of the Peace, Wingate had heard that the Fifth Monarchy Men had suddenly become active in London after a long period of inactivity. Some of the local churchmen thought John Bunyan had Fifth Monarchy sympathies. Perhaps Bunyan's meetings were for hatching plots, or gathering arms. Wingate therefore gave his judgement that John Bunyan had to lie in jail until the next Quarter Sessions in January 1661. He had some final words with his friends, and prayed that he would be kept from all that would dishonour God or discourage the Church. The following day, he was taken under escort twelve miles north to the County jail in Bedford's High Street (on the corner of the present Silver Street). It was around the time of his thirty-third birthday.'

'What kind of life did he have in the prison?' Amy asked.

Andy took time to gather strength and breath. 'Seventeenth century jails were no joke. They weren't like today's prisons, run by the State and regularly inspected. They were filthy, smelly cells, run privately, and full of all manner of abuses. Fees were charged, favours could be bought, and guards could be bribed. Prisoners were overcrowded, sanitary conditions were primitive to say the least, with rampant cross-infection, and forty deaths occurred by plague in Bedford jail in 1665. Many Quaker leaders died in prison. In the winter and early spring of 1660-61 there were more than fifty Quakers in prison with Bunyan. 1665 was the worst year for deaths. During this period, England saw the last wave of bubonic plague to sweep Europe.

'Why bubonic plague?' Amy asked.

'The name came from the buboes, or swollen or inflamed lymph nodes in the armpit or groin. In the fourteenth century it was called the Black Death, because it was spread from China and Central Asia by the fleas from black rats coming on to human beings. It killed between a third and a half of England's population in the fourteenth century within a few months. In the sixteenth century, scholars think it was brought to England by Dutch prisoners-of-war, and killed about a fifth of the population of London (68,000), for example. It was referred to as 'The Great Plague', and was regarded by some (with the Great Fire of London in 1666 and the Dutch Invasion of the Medway in 1667) as a sign of God's anger at the Restoration of the monarchy under Charles II. The Royal Court actually moved out of London for a time.'

'Did the plague reach Bedford?' Amy asked.

'Around forty victims of plague died as it raged around Bedford Jail.'

The authorities acted against the poor at the time of the Great Plague. They were prevented from forming big crowds at funerals by being locked into their homes, and the gentry set up 'pest-houses', often in fields as a means of isolating victims.

'What a good idea!' said Amy with a sparkle. 'Pest-houses! I know a few candidates for one of them! Seriously, was John Bunyan affected?'

Andy continued: 'John Bunyan was exceptionally tough physically, and survived the plague and the freezing winters with God's help. The prison was probably a two-storied building, and had two cells below ground level, one of which had no natural light. There were no fireplaces, and the prisoners slept on straw. John Bunyan had no money to buy any comforts for himself. There were a few concessions. His darling daughter, blind Mary, now eleven years old, would bring in soup from Elizabeth, and the congregation used to bring leather laces for him to tag (put metal tips on for easier insertion in lace-holes). He earned a few pence for the family with this work. At home he had a wife and five children—four of them by his first wife, and a child due to be born before Christmas 1660. When Elizabeth heard that John was arrested, she was so 'smayed (dismayed) at the news' that she went into premature labour, and a week later gave birth to a still-born child.'

'Sometimes, life was not so bad, and later on in his imprisonment an indulgent jailor would let John out. He managed to preach occasionally. My detective hunt in the Bedford Church minute books show that they met as far away as Haynes and Gamlingay, and he preached in woods, fields and isolated farm buildings! He even got as far as London, later on in his imprisonment. In 1666, he was released for a few months, but was re-arrested for preaching!'

'What did he have to read in jail?' Amy asked.

'Well they didn't come round with the book trolley! John Bunyan had only his Bible and concordance, then bought a copy of Foxe's 'Book of Martyrs'. He obtained a copy of William Penn's 'The Sandy Foundations Shaken' (1668) and Edward Fowler's 'The Design of Christianity' (1671). There was a lot of talking and theological discussion, and the brethren took turns preaching to one another on Sundays. Bunyan produced a 294-page book, 'The Holy City' from an expanded sermon based on Revelation chapter 21. It was published in 1665. He was also allowed visitors.'

'Did his friends try to get him out?'

'Of course, Amy. His friends tried, unsuccessfully, to persuade Mr. Crompton, the Justice at Elstow to allow him out on bail. At the January Quarter Sessions, John Bunyan was taken to a gothic-style building known as the Chapel of Herne, which stood on the north bank of the river at the south-west corner of St Paul's churchyard. John Bunyan appeared before a bench of five County Magistrates, all Royalist-sympathising landowners, under Sir John Kelynge of Southill, a practising barrister. This notorious character formed the basis for Bunyan's description of Lord Hate-Good in the trial of Faithful at Vanity Fair, in 'Pilgrim's Progress.' Kelynge was a bitter man with scores to settle against anyone with Puritan sympathies. He had been imprisoned in Windsor Castle from 1642-1660 for royalist activities.

The charge was read out to the prisoner:

'John Bunyan, of the town of Bedford, labourer...hath devilishly and perniciously abstained from coming to church to hear Divine service, and is a common upholder of several unlawful meetings and conventicles, to the great hindrance and distraction of the good subjects of this kingdom contrary to the laws of our sovereign lord, the King.'

Lord Kelynge made a lengthy attack on Bunyan, who proved to be more than a match for him in Biblical argument. Kelynge's judgement was that Bunyan should be returned to prison and given three months to decide to attend Church to hear Divine Service, and to promise to 'leave your preaching', or else be banished from the realm (deported), and if he stayed on in the country, he would 'stretch by the neck for it.'

'He sounds a lovely chap, and I don't think!' said Amy.

'As John Bunyan was being taken out to jail, he told Sir John that if he were out of prison today, he would preach the Gospel again tomorrow by the grace of God.'

'John was dragged away and returned to the prison beside villains, drunks and debtors. On 3 April 1661, the Clerk of the Peace, Mr. Cobb, visited him in prison to bring the magistrates' demand that he should return to the Church of England, and promise to give up his preaching, or things would go badly for him at the next Quarter Sessions.'

When Charles II was crowned, hundreds of prisoners were released as an act of clemency, but Bunyan's name was not included, because local magistrates would have to agree to his release. The April 1661 Quarter-Sessions in Bedford were postponed because of the coronation of King Charles II.

Amy was visibly upset as she asked: 'What happened about his sentence?'

'Time ran out for him. He was now classed as a convicted criminal, and his only hope for pardon was an appeal for clemency during the twelve months after the coronation. There was probably an official conspiracy to keep Bunyan in jail.'

'His wife Elizabeth, grief-stricken at the loss of their first child, and burdened by the responsibility of four small step-children to look after, proved to be a wonderful support to John and the family. John and Elizabeth, probably helped by more educated church members, produced a carefully-worded petition. Several copies were made, and Elizabeth made sure they were distributed.

In the late spring of 1661, she travelled to the House of Lords in London, and presented her petition to Lord Barkwood, a sympathetic peer. After consultation, he told Elizabeth her husband could only be freed at the local Assize hearings.'

'In August 1661, the midsummer Assize was held in the Chapel of Herne, before two Judges, Sir Thomas Twisden and Sir Matthew Hale. Twisden was a hard-nosed Royalist, but Hale had grown up with Dissenters' children, and had sat in Cromwell's Parliament. Elizabeth presented her case to Sir Matthew Hale, and the following day, perhaps unwisely, Elizabeth in desperation threw a copy of the petition through the open window of Twisden's coach. Twisden had his coach stopped and bawled at her saying John Bunyan could not be released until he gave up preaching.'

'So did Elizabeth have to give up her struggle?' Amy asked with great emotion.

'She made one last-ditch, brave attempt. After the Assize, the local gentry generally met with the judges in the Swan Inn (now the Swan Hotel). Elizabeth pushed her way upstairs and burst into the room. She spoke above the noise in a clear and dignified manner, addressing the two judges, explaining that her husband had been falsely accused, and he was not a trouble-maker, so should be released. Hale was again sympathetic, but the local magistrate, Sir Henry Chester of Lidlington, kept reminding the judges that Bunyan had been lawfully convicted. The judges asked her very directly whether her husband was prepared to give up preaching. She said that 'he dares not leave preaching as long as he can breathe.' She explained about her four stepchildren, one of them blind, and how she had lost her own child recently. Twisden said she was using her circumstances to win sympathy. She was told to apply to the King for a pardon, or seek a re-trial. At this, Elizabeth broke down and left the room in tears. She had tried everything.'

'Did they give up after that?' Amy asked anxiously.

'Before the Bedford Assizes of 1662, John tried to have his name entered in the calendar of offenders, so that the judges would have to consider his case. The Clerk of the Peace struck it off, so that Bunyan could remain in prison for the next four years.'

Andy leaned out of the bed to comfort Amy. 'I'm sorry, Amy that you've become so emotionally involved with what started off as a school project. The Bible says 'all things work together for good to those who love God, to those who are called according to His purpose.' (Romans 8 verse 28). In the same section of Paul's Letter to the Romans, the apostle gives a list of disasters, and says 'in all these things we are hyper-conquerors through Him who loved us' (Romans 8 verse 37) Now, I have more bad news for you. The powers that be have told me I have to go to the hospital for a short time. If you feel up to visiting me, that would be very kind. I want you to know that my visit to the hospital has nothing whatever to do with your visits or my detective hunts for information about John Bunyan.'

'I want you to promise me two things. First of all, if you visit me in hospital, we mustn't talk about John Bunyan! Secondly, I want you to promise me that you'll do some homework! While he was in jail, John Bunyan spread his wings as an author. I would like you to write a summary of 'Pilgrim's Progress' within the next month, and we'll take up the John Bunyan story, and see whether you think it had a happy ending!'

'Now raise your right hand, Amy, and say after me 'I, Amy, being of sound mind, will do everything Andy tells me....'

Amy responded immediately, 'Cheerio, you daft thing! I'll see you soon!'

chapter ten

AMY'S HOMEWORK—
PILGRIM'S PROGRESS

Amy sat down and read Pilgrim's Progress, and here is her summary of the story:

THE DREAM
'The author had a dream, concentrated in time, but with lifelong significance. He dreamt about a man like himself, dressed in rags, with a heavy knapsack, and a guidebook, standing by the garden gate. As he read the guidebook, he sweated with terror, and wept with fright, and cried 'What am I going to do?' Although the knapsack was there only as long as he'd been given the guidebook, it was strapped on so tightly he couldn't free himself from it. His parents could neither make sense of his behaviour, nor share his fear. He nearly went mad with the pent-up strain, and his mother couldn't remove the knapsack, or calm him down. Sleep fled from him, and was

replaced by nightmares and dreadful thoughts. His moans and restlessness made neighbours think that he was dying. His father grumbled about his wearing his pack in bed, and Christian finally decided to share the contents of the guidebook with them. He sat them down, and explained to them that they had to leave home to escape the terrible destruction that was coming on their city. His parents tried to pacify him, and treated him as if he were ill, and neighbours came to observe his distressed condition. When they mocked him, or ignored him, he withdrew into himself, and went tramping in the open fields, shouting 'What must I do to be saved?' He would have run away, but he had no clue about which direction to go.

One day he met Evangelist who didn't seem surprised at Christian's problem. Christian told Evangelist he would have to account for his life, character, and the state of his soul. Evangelist gave him a scroll, and told him to obey what it said, that he should run for his life, and head for the City of Gold mentioned in his guidebook. Evangelist told him to read beyond the first chapter, and assured him pilgrims were setting out every day for the City of Gold. Evangelist seemed to lack Christian's urgency and fear, but warned him about the difficulties of the journey. Evangelist also pointed him to a wicket gate and a shining light, and warned him not to lose his scroll. He told him to knock when he reached the gate, and someone would point the way to go. Finally, Evangelist pushed a key into his coat pocket, and said he might need it some day.

Christian ran with all his strength, with his fingers in his ears, past the gaping, grinning, mocking neighbours in their gardens. Two of them actually caught up and ran alongside him, Ob Stinate on his right, and Mr. Bendy on his left, asking loads of questions. When Christian spoke about destruction and the end and condemnation, and tried to persuade them to come with him, Ob Stinate ridiculed him, and refused to leave his home and family, and didn't seem convinced that safety and happiness were better offers, so he slowed down. Mr. Bendy wanted to know more, and stayed with Christian. Ob warned Bendy that he was being led astray, and headed back to the City of Destruction.

THE GREAT BOG MISERY

Christian enjoyed the company of Mr. Bendy, but they ran so fast and talked so much about the glories of the City of Gold, that they failed to notice the bright green, spongy area they came to was a Bog, and they thrashed about in the mud. Bendy ignored Christian's cries for help, and went back the way he had come. Christian felt totally alone and helpless, and was about to drown in the Bog when someone on the firm ground on the far side told him to give him his hand. The stranger introduced himself as Help, and asked why Christian had not used the safe stepping-stones mapped out in the guidebook. Christian asked why the Authorities didn't fill in the Bog, and Help explained the King sent cartloads of advice, wisdom, experience, visions, books, saints art and parables every day, but the Bog was getting bigger and swallowed it all up. As Christian recovered, he saw the cartloads, and realised Help was truthful, and all the fears, worries and troubles of the world dripped into this Great Bog Misery. Help left him to clean up and rest, and said they would perhaps meet again.

Alec Smart knew where the stepping-stones were. He came along, dapper, well-dressed and oozing confidence and experience. He belittled Preacher, and offered to show Christian a short cut to the Celestial City which would take weeks off his journey, and avoid the wicket gate. Alec Smart told him his first job was to get rid of his pack, and asked what was in it. When Christian told him it contained his past and his sins, Alec Smart directed him to a brother and sister of his called Dodge and Quibble, who had an answer for every problem. Unfortunately the path petered out, and he came through a forest to see a steep hillside criss-crossed with identical pathways. The hill towered over him, and Christian thought it was going to fall on him, so he fled. Then he heard the familiar voice of Evangelist asking him why he did not do what he was told, and that he would have to start over again. Christian told Evangelist about Ob Stinate, Bendy and Alec Smart. He almost gave up, but Evangelist encouraged him to retrace his steps by the straight and narrow way, and keep going until the wicket gate. He hoped the Gate Keeper would give him some supper.

THE MUSEUM OF WONDERS

Christian saw the words above the gate: 'Knock and it shall be opened.' He kept on knocking at the gate, and eventually a hand grabbed his wrist and pulled him indoors, just in time to avoid the thud of an arrow striking the gate.

The Gate Keeper explained that the Enemy has archers posted to pick off pilgrims at the door of Pilgrim's Way. He directed Christian to the Museum of Wonders. Christian explained to the Interpreter of the Museum that he had come from the City of Destruction, and was heading for the City of Gold, but he had no money to pay for bed and board, but he was told he could earn his supper by wielding a broom.

The Museum had a magnificent painting in the hall. It was a portrait of a man holding a book and a scroll, looking upwards into a beam of light. He had a saintly face and a smile. When Christian asked Interpreter what it meant, he was told this man was one in a million. His work was to know and unfold dark things to sinners. The world was cast behind him, and he despised things of this world, and has hope of glory to come.

A broom was thrust into his hand, and Christian was told to sweep up in a small dark room. The whole room was covered in a thick layer of dust, and as soon as he started sweeping, huge clouds of it blew up and choked Christian, making him sneeze. The more he moved, the more the room was engulfed in dust. Suddenly, a young woman came in and without a word started to dip her fingers in a bowl of water and sprinkle the room with droplets. The dust settled at once, and in a short time she was able to sweep a heap of dust and ash back in the fireplace.

The Interpreter said that they dealt in allegory there, and the young lady's name was Gospel. The room represented the heart of someone who has not heard the Good News. The more he thinks of wickedness, the more he multiplies wickedness and doubts, and he feels even worse. That was when he needed the Gospel most, to prove that Good will always triumph over Bad in the end. Christian realised he had become an exhibit himself! Christian asked to see more, but the Interpreter ordered him to rest, and promised he would see everything, and had just to watch, without taking part.

The Museum had a great collection of automata, moving models with repeated activities. Christian ran from one to another, but needed the Interpreter to explain everything.

For instance, there were two children at a table, one patient, the other noisily impatient for his food. A hatch opened, and a plate was served to the wriggler who gobbled it down, mocking the quiet child. When the quiet child was served, however much he ate the plate was refilled with delicious food. The Curator explained that the children were Patience and Passion. The two lads were two types. Passion wants happiness right away, but if it comes it doesn't last; it is suddenly gone. Patience waits for happiness, and when it comes, it lasts.

The next model was of a fire with real flames! A nasty crowd of small men in red suits were pouring buckets of water on the flames, yet the fire kept burning. When Christian asked about it, the Interpreter led him to the side of the machine, where he could see an oil can with a long nozzle was always feeding the fire with oil. The Interpreter explained it was not a trick. The fire represented all a pilgrim can achieve when he sets his mind to it. The Enemy will try to stop him. The oil-can represents God.

The Christian was shown a man in an iron cage, with a sad expression. His eyes were downcast, and he sighed as if he were heartbroken. Interpreter encouraged Christian to talk with him, and he discovered he had once been a pilgrim, but had become shut up in the iron cage of despair. He had repeatedly spurned the Son of God, and there was no hope for him. All the passions, pleasures and advantages of the world were biting him, and gnawing him like a burning worm. Interpreter told Christian to remember the man's misery as a perpetual warning.

The Museum had glass cases with a variety of ancient objects—a tent-peg, a slingshot and five pebbles, the jawbone of an ass, a basket made of bulrushes, some locks of hair, a brick made without straw. Each item was a reminder of a story from the guidebook. The people who owned them were pilgrims themselves once.

Another automaton showed a palace with a fierce guard at one end. People crowded round the door, their knees knocking with fear for the guarded door. There was a man seated at a table with a book and a pen, taking the names of people who could enter the palace. Then a lad came in wearing a helmet and a breastplate and a very determined expression. 'Write my name down, sir,' he said to the man at the entrance. Without warning, the armed man suddenly drew a short sword and rushed at the guard. After a fierce skirmish the guard sat down hard, and the lad leaped over him and pressed forward into the palace.

Don't tell me!' Christian said 'The boy is Bravery. You have to take courage and take action to win through.'

'You do know allegory' said the Curator.

Christian, he was wearing what I need—armour!'

'You'll pass the Armoury down the road,' said the Interpreter.

When Christian asked whether there were any more exhibits, he was told there was only one, which was rather scary.

The end room of the Museum was in total darkness. Christian saw outlines of his home town, threatened by black clouds and a blood-red moon, crumbling mountains, with molten lava engulfing it. There were moving figures in red and white, like two battle lines being drawn up, and troops gathering. The white troops in the sky seemed to descend into the town at their commander's orders, and were cheered by some while others cringed in terror. Two doors opened, one full of fire and one full of light and music. A tidal wave swept Christian off his feet, and only a pearly pool remained where his town had been.

Interpreter was at the Museum door as Christian left. He knew that it was no allegory he had seen—it was the End of the World. Interpreter told him to take all these things to heart, so that they would spur him on in his travels.

THE HILL AND THE CROSS

High walls lined the Pilgrim's Way beyond the Museum of Wonders, and Christian saw a man and a woman scaling the wall on to the path. They were called Miss Stake and Mr. Smug, and explained they had come the quick way, avoiding the wicket gate. They had no scrolls, or knapsack, and said the great thing was to be in, no matter how you got there. Christian remembered the Curator's words to keep the scroll, which was a passport into the City of Gold, and keep to the straight and narrow way. They were very sure and very speedy, and reached the hill long before Christian did. The Hill was very steep, and skull-shaped, and at its foot the lane split in three in the shadow of a signpost—east, west and straight up. The paths to right and left were smooth, broad and flower-strewn.

Miss Stake and Mr. Smug quarrelled about which direction to take, then took east and west in opposite directions. This time Christian would keep to the straight and narrow, even when it was steep and narrow. Further up the Hill, Christian got a better perspective. The west path petered out and the east path led into thick woods, and there was no sign of Miss Stake or Mr. Smug.

At the top of the hill he saw three wooden crosses sunk into the ground, with blood-stained nails sticking out at awkward angles.

At the top of the middle cross a notice read 'King of the Jews.' Then the notice seemed to change to 'Light of the World', then 'The Truth and the Way', and 'The Door.' The cross was a brutal instrument of execution on which a man had been nailed up to die.

Christian tried to imagine what it would have been like to be there. His head couldn't cope, and he fell to his knees. Suddenly, there was a 'thwack', and his load fell off his back, and rolled down the far side of the slope. He ran after it, and it rolled downhill into a kind of burial cave with its rock door rolled back. He could see nothing inside the cave. Three Shining Ones came to him. The first one said 'your sins are forgiven.' The second one stripped him of his rags and dressed him in a fresh set of clothes. The third one set a mark on his forehead, and gave him a scroll with a seal on it. He was told to look at the scroll as he ran, and hand it in at the gate of the City of Gold. Christian gave three jumps for joy, and went on his way singing. He sat down under a leafy shelter with a bench and a fruit tree and a drinking fountain, specially provided for pilgrims. Still no sign of Miss Stake or Mr. Smug. Christian fell into a deep sleep perfectly relaxed.

THE LIONS

In his dreams, Jesus had been saying 'Could you not stay awake one hour? Stay awake and pray!' Then he heard shrill voices complaining about the size and the teeth of something they had seen, and saw a man and a woman running pell-mell towards him. Christian told them the Golden City was in the other direction, and the man said he could keep it—they were going back. The woman agreed –'Hardship is one thing, but lions is another!' she said. Tim Id and Miss Trust were chattering with fright. Within half a mile, Christian could hear the echoing sound of lions roaring. He wondered whether his scent would carry that far. Then he saw two of them, crouched, noses on their paws. They bared their yellow teeth. Christian's resolve melted away at the sight of those teeth. Then a voice said, 'Have faith...just have faith, Christian.' It was Faithful. Christian wondered why the King would set the beasts there. Faithful called: 'Just walk through! They won't hurt you!' Faithful was beyond the lions, calling to him. Christian remembered Bravery and walked on. The lions lunged, but two strong metal chains pulled them up short, and Christian walked through, unharmed.

Christian ran after Faithful, and they walked close together, sharing stories. Christian learned Faithful had lived just a few doors down from him in the City of Destruction. He had been there when Bendy returned, and began bad-mouthing Christian, but no one listened. Some said he was a coward for giving up, and some said he was for running away in the first place! He lost the trust of his business colleagues and his wife. He locked himself in his attic, and wouldn't come out. Christian learned that his own parents were planning to set out soon for the City of Gold.

THE ARMOURY

Just then, the Armoury came into view, a bleak building with brilliant light shining from its windows. Faithful pulled out his scroll, and Christian had the awful realisation he had dropped his scroll. He retraced his steps, past the threatening lions in the gathering darkness. He searched carefully all over the area where he had rested, and found the scroll under the bench at the leafy shelter. 'Evangelist warned me not to fall asleep, to be watchful and stay awake....I'll never sleep again!' Christian was back at the Armoury door within two hours. Would there be anyone to open the door? A woman's voice told him he was very late, and they were beginning to be concerned about him.

Christian expected a tough, experienced soldier to be in charge of the Armoury, but found three quiet, friendly girls there—Prudence, Patience and Charity. They brought Christian a lovely supper, and led him to a bedroom called Peace, and he had the best sleep ever.

During the next day, the three girls showed Christian the ancient records of the Lord of the Hill, and read some of the noble acts performed by some of the Lord's servants, and told how willing the Lord was to receive anyone into his service.

Next morning the women took him to a heap of shining fighting gear, provided by the Lord for pilgrims, and he chose a breastplate, helmet, sword and shield, and tough-wearing boots.

The girls told him his boots would never wear out, and that he should put on his armour—the sword-belt of Truth, the breastplate of Righteousness, the shield of Faith, the helmet of Salvation, and the sword of the Spirit. Christian started searching for a backplate, and was told they didn't issue them, because anyone who turned their back on the enemy was doomed.

When Christian saw his image with his armour on in the window-pane, he felt privileged to be a footsoldier of the King. A ragamuffin had been transformed into a warrior! Before he set out again on his journey, they told him Faithful had passed by, and Christian met up with him again.

APOLLYON THE MONSTER

As they travelled across the pleasant countryside, Christian reflected that Faithful had done better than he had, not losing his scroll, or falling in the Bog, or being misled by Alec Smart. He had also passed the lions without knowing that they were chained. Faithful told him how he had also been close to disaster. He had met an old man who admired Faithful so much, he offered him a job as manager of his estate, since he had no son, only three lovely daughters. At dinner, Faithful, couldn't keep his eyes off these beautiful girls—black-haired, blonde and red-headed. They turned on their feminine charms, and when he spoke to the old man, he was offered all three if he wished! When he was praying that night, his room door opened. He caught a glimpse of a pair of handcuffs in the moonlight, and it dawned on him that the old man's wealth was based on slavery! Faithful noticed that Christian was encouraged to think that he wasn't the only pilgrim to make mistakes...He was indulging himself on congratulations when Faithful cried out, and ran past him, pursued by a dreadful monster. It had wings like a dragon, feet like a bear, and the mouth of a lion. It was covered in fish scales, and fire and smoke spurted noisily out of its navel.

It roared at Christian: 'Stand still, petty subject, and name yourself! Are you not a runaway slave of mine?' The monster stood barring his way forward.

'I used to serve someone like you, but my new name is Christian, and my new Master is King of this land.'

The monster claimed Christian was his because he was within his borders. Christian said he wanted to leave his borders to go to the City of Gold. Apollyon ordered him to stay and serve him. When Christian said he liked neither the pay nor the job prospects, Apollyon promised improvement and power-sharing, Christian said he now fought under a different King, against whose forces, Apollyon had no power.

Apollyon reminded Christian of his failures so far and the hopelessness of his prospects of making the City of Gold. Christian told of his new King's forgiveness, which inspired his loyalty, and Apollyon threatened to spill his soul.

Christian drew his sword, and resolved to fight to the death. Apollyon hurled fiery darts at him, and Christian used his shield to deflect them. Then Apollyon got him in a stranglehold, and almost bashed his brains out, so his helmet fell off, and set about stripping him of his armour. They wrestled in hand-to-hand combat for an hour, so Christian's energy was sapped, then Apollyon raised his paw to rip out his heart. Christian found the hilt of his sword, and thrust it upwards into the monster's belly, below its ribs. Apollyon's fire subsided, and his mighty wings carried him off, covering his wound with one paw.

In a moment, Faithful was at Christian's side, tending his wounds with Leaves from the Tree of Life. Faithful congratulated him, but Christian knew Apollyon was attracted by the smell of pride from him. They rested under the Tree of Life, and as they recuperated, Evangelist came and sat alongside them. He told them it was time for one of them to end his journey, and one of them to go on.

They underlined their intention to travel together all the way, but Preacher said there was trouble and danger ahead, and one of them would pay the fare for the only quick route to the City of Gold. As they jingled their money, Evangelist said either of them could pay: the fare had to be paid in blood. The time had come for one of them to die!

VANITY FAIR

Christian and Faithful walked on, with Evangelist's words reverberating in their ears. Who was going to die?

Pilgrim's Way suddenly took them into the middle of a huge fairground, Vanity Fair, which had been going for five thousand years. Many of the traders had started off as pilgrims, and never got any further.

Vanity Fair was a sprawling mess of colourful canvas, and noisy, busy hustlers, touting for trade twenty-four hours a day. Litter blew around everywhere, and there was never any shortage of customers. The goods on display came from all over the world, and included everything to eat, or wear or admire. Wives could be bought and traded, and vast land deals were on offer. Titles and trophies could be purchased, and the restless traders were always on the move to bigger and better pitches. Games and contests of all sorts were there, and all kinds of jobs on offer. Everything seemed cheap and nasty to Christian and Faithful, whose hearts were focussed on the City of Gold. They bought nothing, and gradually they noticed that the din had become louder, noise and the shouting were being directed at them. Mockery gave way to open hostility, especially when Faithful said, when pressed, that they had nothing that he was after. When a fishwife asked 'what DO they want?', Faithful asked for a basket of Truth, if they had it! When that happened, the pilgrims were manhandled on to a barrow and trundled through the streets. They were beaten, put into a cage on wheels, and wheeled through the Fair to suffer physical and verbal abuse. Disagreements about the pilgrims erupted into fisticuffs. They noticed a bright-faced girl, who was an interested spectator. The site manager appeared and said they would be on trial the next day for disturbing the peace.

Christian and Faithful said their prayers and bedded down in the straw, making the best of their cage. The noise of the Fair continued, of course.

In the morning they were dragged into a makeshift courtroom, with the Fair Manager, Lord Hate-Good, as Judge. A salesman with a sword said they had caused a disturbance by belittling Vanity Fair, and looking without buying, and not caring about his knighthoods.

They complained about them looking different. They made false witness against them, then the bright-eyed girl, whose name was Hopeful, said they had done nothing wrong. She pointed out that there was not a basket of Truth to be had in Vanity Fair.

Hopeful's speech incensed the Judge, who condemned Faithful to be put to death, and that his death should be as miserable as possible. Christian roared out for justice and a retrial, but Faithful was dragged away. When he heard screaming, Christian prayed for him. Then he discovered they had left the cage door unlocked, and it swung open. Christian found the brutalised body of Faithful lying in the mud where his murderers had left it. The Fair had quieted down, and Christian heard the voice of Hopeful, the bright-faced girl, offering to travel on with him. He asked her whether Faithful had said anything before he died. She said Faithful had commented that Jesus Christ had walked through Vanity Fair, once, and he bought nothing either. They were interrupted by the thunderous noise of a horse-drawn chariot roaring through the Fair. The charioteer halted the horses close to Faithful's head, and he took Faithful's hand and led him into the chariot.

His body and clothing became transparent, and the horses whisked him away into the morning sky. The City of Gold was near enough Vanity Fair for him to be home by sunset.

Christian asked Hopeful whether they were the only people who prized their journey more than the trinkets Vanity Fair had to offer. She told him others would follow, but many had been dazzled and sidetracked by it. Christian looked up, and murmured to Faithful to keep a place for him.

FILTHY LUCRE

Two pilgrims called Natter Jack and Owen Ends caught up with them on the road. Natter Jack seemed a good conversationalist, and Owen Ends seemed very spiritual. But Natter Jack was an incessant talker about every subject under the sun. He never listened to anyone else, or seemed to take time to think, or even to draw breath! Christian valued silence after listening to him. Natter Jack knew the contents of Christian's guidebook thoroughly, but he was very opinionated about every subject in the book. His voice was like needles jabbing their brain, so they were very grateful when he went off in a huff because Christian disagreed with him on some issue. Owen Ends made Christian feel uneasy, because he seemed to have had a perfectly trouble-free pilgrimage. This smooth and cool man had used his religious advantages to charm women, attract business and finance people, win social and legal high office, and it all came down to religious respectability. His success showed in his expensive clothes. He was totally flummoxed when Christian asked whether he believed in his religion, for his emphasis was on correct performance rather than faith.

Then they heard the clatter of machinery over the hill, and among the dust clouds beside the road they saw a man in a very fancy waistcoat. He was waving at them to come and see a new seam they had discovered in the high-grade silver mine in Lucre Hill.

His name was Pluto Crat, the Chief Engineer, and he was promising life-time riches for a few hours of work. Christian apologised because they had no time to spare, but Hopeful wanted to see the mine, and both she and Owen Ends were enthusiastic about the good they could do with wealth. Owen Ends was charmed to bits, and went off with Pluto Crat. Christian pleaded, successfully, with Hopeful to spy out the place. They scrambled up the side of the hill and were astounded when they saw that the other side had been sliced away, so that Lucre Hill was a dangerous cliff, with groups of men roped together and hacking away at the cliff face, without any concern for those around them. Dark tunnels had been bored into the base of the hill, and gangs of miners , men and women chained together, engaged in the back-breaking work. Hopeful was amazed at the level of activity which made them seem like slaves or convicts, driven on by the hope of getting rich quickly. From their hiding-place they saw Owen Ends with Pluto Crat in the distance, and to their horror they saw Owen Ends over-reaching, and falling down the cliff face to his death. The noise of the machinery and the concentration of the workers meant the work continued without interruption, and Pluto Crat sauntered back to the highway to look for more prospects.

Hopeful and Christian were back on the Way quickly, Hopeful full of running power and gratitude for Christian's help. Christian conceded that money could do a lot of good in the world, but said that getting it was an energy-sapping exercise that could tear your heart out. They settled for a night's sleep in a flower-strewn meadow beside a stream, and it was Christian's idea because the path seemed to go in the same direction as Pilgrim's Way. They were wakened by the earth trembling, and a terrifyingly loud voice roaring:

> *'Earth, salt, fire, and brim!*
> *I smell the blood of a true pilgrim!*
> *If any trespass hereabout*
> *He'll end his days in Castle Doubt!*

DOUBTING CASTLE

They were in the food-less, waterless dungeon of Doubting Castle, Christian wailed in the darkness that it was all his fault.

They should never have left the Pilgrim Pathway. At last the door swung open and the amazingly ugly Giant stood there and mocked them when Christian said they were friends and that their King would save them. The Giant said no-one knew where they were, they had left the King's Highway, and given themselves into his power. Their King had died two thousand years earlier, and there was no Golden City. When they explained they were of no value for ransom purposes, and asked why he was keeping them, he said he was keeping them to kill them, although he would prefer them to commit suicide. When he reported to his huge ugly slob of a wife that

Hopeful said they were not afraid, she told the Giant to beat them with his club. Next time he came, he gave them a severe beating, and advised suicide. The candle he left lit up a rope, a knife, and a bottle of poison. Hopeful shouted after the Giant that they had been in tighter spots, and the King had helped them. He beat them up the next day, again advising suicide. Hopeful said no true pilgrim would kill himself, but the beating left them longing for Death. The Giant's wife moaned because the Enemy wouldn't pay them their reward unless the Pilgrims despaired. Next day, on his wife's advice, they were taken, chained, to see the bleached bones of those who had died in Doubting Castle. Hopeful again said 'Where there's life, there's hope!' When they got back to the cell, every ledge was full of jars of poison. The Giant gloated over his joke that it wasn't every jailor who gives his prisoner the key to escape.

Suddenly, Christian remembered the key which Evangelist had given him with the book and the scroll, and which he had forgotten. There were words etched along the barrel of the key which read:

> 'And lo, I am with you always,
> even unto the end of the world.'

It turned out the key fitted the dungeon and the exit gate, and there was no sign of Mr. or Mrs. Giant, so they ran back to the Pilgrim's Way, and wrote a warning on a big boulder:

> 'Here be giants
> Nearby stands Doubting Castle.
> Do NOT stray from the path.'

THE DELECTABLE MOUNTAINS

Suddenly Christian and Hopeful found themselves in the flower-strewn foothills of snow-capped mountains, with sheep grazing everywhere. The bells around their necks made lovely music as they moved. Shepherds sat round a wood fire playing pipes and whistles. It all seemed too good to be true, but the shepherds reassured them by telling them they were on the King's ground, the Delectable Mountains, and they were seeing the King's sheep and his shepherds. The pilgrims were given fresh nourishing food, and invited to share the shepherds hut that night with two other pilgrims. Christian wondered who they were. Christian and Hopeful were invited to view the way back, and when they agreed, they were shown an iron gate in the hillside which led to a black chute falling away into oblivion. The shepherd said some pilgrims got within sight of the Golden City, only to end their journey there. Christian asked whether they were within sight of the Golden City, and the shepherds gave them a telescope, and told them which way to look. All they could see was a shimmering brightness. The shepherds' hut had good food and comfortable beds, and Christian recognised Mr. Smug and Miss Stake, and introduced them to Hopeful. They had avoided danger and destruction, but they had no scrolls to present at the Golden City. Hopeful was dismayed at The views of the other two that the important thing was to be on the Way, and to travel light.

Christian and Hopeful wakened early and Christian wanted to be off without the other two, who made him feel uneasy. The shepherds warned them against setting out alone, and told how a gang of bandits had recently robbed someone called Little Faith, and barely stopped short of killing him, had they not thought the King's Champion was coming. He had no money to buy food, and all he had left was his scroll. Smug was awake to hear the story, and said he could have sold his book or scroll, but they said he went hungry, was haunted with fear and doubt, and thought he just wasn't meant to reach the Golden City. Little Faith didn't have the courage that others had to whistle for the King's Champion.

As the four pilgrims walked on, Christian told them that his friend Faithful would have whistled immediately, but Christian said he was too much like Little Faith. At this, Smug ridiculed Christian, and praised his own merits and intelligence. Hopeful wasn't sure whether she would whistle, but would like to see the King's Champion on the way. Suddenly, there was the thunder of hooves, and the King's Champion and escort appeared, and only Smug was left as the rest scattered. The chain the escorts carried encircled him, and he was taken to the door on the hillside, and posted down the chute to Nothingness. 'So his road did lead to Destruction, after all,' Hopeful murmured. Miss Stake wasn't unduly put out by his loss, and said he was a fool, anyway.

AMBUSH

As they travelled, they came to a fork in the road, with no signpost. There was an Irishman sitting, who said the Golden City would be privileged to have such fine pilgrims. Miss Stake was very suspicious, and said he was a beggar. He pointed the way, and said they were so experienced they could sense the right way. Miss Stake went off to the left, in the opposite direction, and O'Flattery showered them with compliments, and invited them home. Suddenly, they found themselves snared into a net, and suspended in the air between two trees. O'Flattery began to insult them for believing good about themselves, and promised them a harsh lesson on humility. Neither of them could summon up a whistle for the King's Champion. Along came a ragged man who cut them down. He denied there was a right path, and a City of Gold, and told them he was once like them, but he had given up and had been on his travels for fifty years. Atheist also denied there was a King, and an Enemy, and a Hell, and they could tell from his hollow laughter that he was engulfed in bitterness.

THE ENCHANTED GROUND

The pilgrims encountered a persistent, enchanting cloud of drowsiness rising from the poppy fields as they passed. Hopeful said they should lie down and rest, but Christian spurred her on, and put an encouraging arm round her, and told her to sing so that they could both stay awake. They sang:

'He who would valiant be 'gainst all disaster
let him in constancy follow the Master!
There's no discouragement
Shall make him once relent
His first avowed intent
To be a pilgrim!

'Whoso beset him round with dismal stories,
do but themselves confound; his strength the more is!

No foes shall stay his might,
Though he with giants fight:
He will make good the right
To be a pilgrim!

They used riddles and quizzes to keep themselves awake, until suddenly Christian tripped over the sleeping form of Miss Stake. They carried her clear of the edge of the poppy field, and carried on into beautiful bandit-free, enchantment-free country, singing:

'Then fancies flee away!
I'll fear not what men say,
I'll labour night and day
To be a pilgrim!

THE VALLEY OF THE SHADOW

The following days were the sweetest days of their pilgrimage, walking through the Land of Beulah, their hearts aching with happiness as their joy increased. Christian noticed the signs of ageing in Hopeful. They walked slowly until they found themselves surrounded by rocks, and enclosed in a freezing and fearful glen, where the wind howled and the sun was shut out by black clouds. The only light came from lightning flashes and fires raging on the slopes.

The worst noise in the Valley of the Shadow was the cumulative noise of crying from myriads of sick people— diseased, delirious and insane; war casualties moaning for help, the drowning and the starving, including children, and the dying, crying 'Why me?

Some complained about the King. The path had become a very narrow causeway, with deep trenches on either side. The only thing to do was to keep to the path, and pray constantly. Hopeful went through agonies, wanting to help, but unable to stretch across the trenches. They prayed:

'Yea, though I walk through the Valley of the Shadow of Death, I will fear no evil; for thou art with me; thy rod and thy staff they comfort me. Surely goodness and mercy shall follow me all the days of my life; and I will dwell in the house of the Lord for ever.'

Praying brought them through, and the glen gave way to beautiful, colourful, cultivated countryside. They plucked clusters of grapes from the vines. An increasing volume of noise reached Christian's ears, that of a rushing river. Hopeful gasped and pointed 'There it is, Christian! The City! We've arrived!'

The brilliance they saw beamed from the walls of the City of Gold, whose outline was clearly visible. They ran together, and suddenly the Pilgrim's Way ended at the river-bank. There was no bridge across the Final River!

The voice of a white-coated farmer encouraged them to cross over. In answer to their questions, he said the river depth varied, according to their faith in surviving. Hopeful slid into the River, and the water came up to her neck, and Christian followed her in. He lost breath, and found weed instead of pebbles under his feet. His head was submerged, and Hopeful responded to his cries for help by encouraging him to come nearer her. He tried in vain to climb out again. He went over near a ferry-boat when he saw Miss Stake being helped in to it by a cloaked and hooded ferryman, then he saw the name of the boat, 'Vain Hope.' When the ferryman heard that she had no scroll, he pushed the boat off, and the boat capsized. Miss Stake was swept away in the current. Christian plunged from the bank, out of his depth, while Hopeful encouraged him to reach for her hand, and keep looking at the City, and reminding him the pilgrims had further to go after Death. Although he saw the City, he was being swept away, but Hopeful waded over and, supporting his head, drew him through the water. Suddenly, hands reached out and lifted them ashore.

Teams of angels wrapped them and dried them. Their hair and features had changed, as if the River had washed away all sorrow and hardship pain and age. The River had stripped off their armour, and wrenched their guidebooks form their grasp, and all they had left was their tight grip on their blemish-free scrolls.

The angel-guard who inspected their scrolls welcomed them home at last. The place was thronged with people drinking in an air of celebration and fun. There was joyful dancing, and they joined in. There were sweet smells of roses and food cooking. They saw Little Faith and Faithful greeted them with the news that Christian's mother and father had arrived weeks ago. They were enclosed in a spirit of eternal, godly leisure.

The Dreamer could not describe what Christian saw when he came face to face with the King, or what Hopeful saw when her hopes were fulfilled. The Dreamer awoke. He will have to find out for himself the wonders of the City of Gold, for he like all of us, is on a pilgrimage.

chapter eleven

JOHN BUNYAN IN PRISON

A my had been a regular enough visitor during the two weeks that Andy spent in the hospital. She had also obeyed the rules by not talking about John Bunyan. She waited for two weeks after she knew he was home, and then went on her fact-finding mission.

Before she came to visit Andy, Amy's family had a visit from Andy's Mum. She explained that she didn't want to talk about Andy when he was around, but was free to tell them about the relentless routine of pounding him in different positions to clear up the mucus which clogged up his lungs. He was always on drugs, and had recently been on oral antibiotics. The reason for his admission to the hospital was that his Mum had noticed with alarm that his face, hands and ankles had begun to swell. Andy was beginning to retain fluid. During his stay in the hospital, they were able to give Andy relief by oxygen supply, and were able to balance his drugs, and then to strengthen the dosage after observing his condition. The only long-term cure for his breathlessness would be a lung transplant.

When Amy visited Andy, after saying the hellos, it was down to business:

'I see you did your homework, Amy!'

'Yes, 'Teach', I did and I hope you have been able to read over the work,' Amy replied.

'Yes, Amy, and thank you for that fine effort.' Andy looked rather embarrassed.

'When did John Bunyan write 'Pilgrim's Progress?' she asked.

'The point is did you enjoy it?' Andy hit back with a question.

'Yes, I did! But I enjoyed it much better when I cheated, and read it in a modern version!'

'Have you any questions?'

'Yes, I've got loads of questions about it. Is it true Bunyan wrote it while he was in prison?'

'Yes, Amy, he did. He stayed in jail and let his mind wander. He didn't write it during the first long imprisonment, but during a second term in prison, for six months in 1676. It was published in February 1678. He wrote the second part later on, in 1684.'

'What do you think are the main truths he is trying to get across? Is this the Thinker bit?'

'Well, Amy, prisoners certainly get time to think. Some daren't, or their thoughts would destroy them. For others, prison is a time to explore their inner selves, and find out what they are really like. Dag Hammerskjold, a former Secretary General of the United Nations, said: 'the longest journey is the journey inward. What makes Bunyan so healthy an author to read, is that having thought out his position, he sets out his basic principles in a good story, which even children can read.

'What are these principles?' Amy asked. 'And do you have to be clever to understand them?'

Andy continued: 'It's a bit like the parables of Jesus. Remember how Jesus said 'he that has ears to hear, let him hear. The storyteller had a vital part to play in a society without books, newspapers, mobile telephones, radio and television.' Parables were a means of sifting the hearers, to separate out those with a genuine interest in spiritual things, who were searching for God.'

John Bunyan actually used our Lord's teaching by parables as an argument against people who did not want him to publish 'Pilgrim's Progress.' They thought it would just confuse the readers. Bunyan thought the principles in the story were valid and true to life.

The first principle is that we're all on a spiritual journey, heading for the heart's true home. The journey is the most accurate picture of human life. Second, we have a guidebook. Third, we will encounter all sorts of individuals on the journey —some friendly, some hostile. Fourth, like Christian in the story, we all have to face a variety of obstacles and difficulties —bogs to traverse and mountains to climb. Fifth, our greatest burden through life is our wrongdoing and sin. Sixth, we are not left to struggle alone—we are given helpers on the journey. Seventh, God has kindly made provision to deal with that biggest burden through the Cross of Jesus, our Saviour, who as our Sin-bearer can lift the burden from us, and come to us as God's Champion when we cry to him for help on the journey.'

'I'll tell you what I was wondering about as I was doing that Homework you gave me,' said Amy. 'Have the people who know, like yourself, managed to link up the places in the book with actual places in the Bedford area?'

'There have been many judicious conjectures, (other people call them 'guesses', Amy) said Andy, some more definite than others.'

'John Gifford's rectory, on the east side of John Street, Bedford, has often been linked with the Museum of Wonders, or Interpreter's House. The Cross and the Empty Tomb have been linked with the fourteenth century cross in the village of Stevington, six miles east of Bedford. The Hill Difficulty has been pinpointed as Greensands Ridge, that part of the Chiltern Hills which enters the village of Ampthill, six miles south of Bedford. The Delectable Mountains would have to be identified as the Chiltern Hills, the highest area around Bedford. Vanity Fair is clearly linked with the village green at Elstow. Other places are not so clearly identified, like the Great Bog Misery, which could be any one of several marshy areas around. Although many of the areas have been drained, the best guess is the area between Elstow and Harrowden, to the right of the road past the entrance to the Abbey School. The Valley of the Shadow of Death has been linked to the tree-lined gorge near the village of Millbrook, south of Bedford.'

'When we tackle the ideas in the book, there are some links with Bunyan's life, times and opponents. He knew all about burdens—every day he was away from home plying his trade as a tinker, he had to carry a bag of tools, including a portable anvil. The notion of Christian going through the agonies did echo Bunyan's experience, but they are also standard teaching in Puritan terms.

Many modern Christians would see a variety of ways in which God brings us to faith. They would say being 'born again' is a bit like being born. It is not a uniform pattern of experience. Some babies are born in crisis, while others are born quietly and naturally with the minimum of pain and difficulty. In the New Testament (Acts chapter 16), the jailer comes to faith through an earthquake, but Lydia's heart was opened by the Lord like a flower to the sunlight. The pilgrimage, like coming to faith, is a combination of ups and downs—there is the Great Bog Misery, The Hill Difficulty, Doubting Castle and the Valley of the Shadow as well as the 'good bits'—the hospitality of Interpreter's House and the joys of the Delectable Mountains.

At the scene where he loses his burden, it is neither a cross nor a crucifix that saves Christian. There is no pardon in a lump of wood. That is why he says:

'Blest cross, blest sepulchre, blest rather be
The man who there was put to shame for me.'

Bunyan is perhaps correcting any superstition about religious objects which was a sign of his times as well as ours.

'What were the most important lessons Bunyan learned in prison?' Amy asked.

Andy said 'I think trust in God, patience with his cramped circumstances, and tolerance towards those who did not share his views. He had to learn increasingly to look to God to care for Elizabeth and the children. He did what he could to earn money to support them, but he trusted more and more in God's care for them and himself. In his cramped circumstances, he learned to make the best of his life, and turn fences into ladders whenever he could. The Bunyan Museum displays a wooden flute which John was supposed to have produced in prison, by hollowing out the leg of a stool, and burning the holes with his candle flame! His character must have impressed prison guards if some of them were willing to let him out, and believe his promise to come back! In prison, he found himself in embarrassingly close contact with religious opponents. His early writings include two very strong pamphlets written against the Quakers, and he found himself in jail with crowds of Quakers. His respect for them grew as he saw them enduring the same suffering and indignity as himself. There is some evidence that his views and dealings with them changed over the years, and they gained more respect from John Bunyan.'

Amy gave Andy an old-fashioned look as she asked him: My Granddad used to say 'the pen is mightier than the sword.' Would you say this was true in John Bunyan's life?'

'Definitely, Amy! Martin Luther used to talk about his little lead soldiers winning many battles—he meant the letters of the alphabet in type-set. John Bunyan's books made him famous and had a far-reaching influence. By the time he was forty, his books were being read by large numbers of people. He probably began writing 'Pilgrim's Progress' before his release from prison in 1672, and finished part I during his six-months in prison in 1676. It was published in 1678. Historically, it was easier for Bunyan to publish it in 1678 than in 1676. The brief period of tolerance which followed Charles II's Declaration of Indulgence in 1672 was followed by a new wave of persecution which didn't die down until 1678. Bunyan also had theological hesitations about publishing a fictional work on such a serious subject, and wondered how the serious-minded Christians would react to it. Certainly, his scheme of interspersing exciting narrative with wholesome conversations was a winner, just as it was with Cervantes' 'Don Quixote' earlier. There was also a good publishing reason. Bunyan's London connections were flourishing, and he switched to Nathaniel Ponder, John Owen's publisher, who could give the book wider circulation. Within ten years of its publication, it passed through ten editions, selling a remarkable one hundred thousand copies! Before Bunyan died, it had been translated into several other European languages. The story has become an international classic, and has been published in over two hundred languages throughout the world. Bunyan earned very little from the sale of his books. When he died, his estate was worth about fifty pounds, yet he has left the world a great legacy of writing.

'Did he write any books other than 'Pilgrim's Progress' in prison?' Amy asked.

'He was very busy as a writer. 'I Will Pray with the Spirit' was written in 1662/63. 'Prison Meditations' (a book of poems), 'Christian Behaviour' is dated 1663, and 'A Map, Showing the Order and Causes of Salvation and Damnation' was possibly written in 1663. 1665 was a busy year for writing—'One Thing is Needful', 'Ebal and Gerizzim', 'The Holy City', and possibly 'The Resurrection of the Dead' were all written then. His testimony story, 'Grace Abounding to the Chief of Sinners' is dated 1666, and 'The Heavenly Footman' was possibly written in 1671. 'A Defence of the Doctrine of Justification by Faith' was dated 1672. In total, he wrote over sixty books! To complete the story, some of his more well-known books were 'Pilgrim's Progress, Part I' (1676), 'Come, and Welcome, to Jesus Christ' (1681), 'The Life and Death of Mr. Badman' (1680), now known as 'The Road to Hell'(1680),'The Holy War' (1682), about the spiritual warfare the Christian has to face in his life. It features Mansoul, Captain Anything, Mr. God's Peace and Diabolus (the Devil), and Emmanuel. 'Pilgrim's Progress, Part II' was written in 1684-5. The second part of 'Pilgrim's Progress' traces the pilgrimage of Christian's wife Christiana, and her children, whom he had left behind when he fled from the City of Destruction. They follow a dream, too, and travel with their neighbour Mercy, and receive help from Great-Heart, who defeats Giant Despair and other assorted enemies. Mr. Honest, Mr. Despondency and his daughter Much-Afraid, Mr. Steadfast, and Mr. Valiant-for-Truth are all involved in the journey. The words of the well-known hymn 'Who would true valour see' are in this Part of 'Pilgrim's Progress.'

In the last year of his life, he wrote no fewer than five books, including 'The Jerusalem Sinner Saved', and 'The Acceptable Sacrifice'. The manuscript for this last book was in his pocket on his final journey to London.'

'Well, Andy, I mustn't tire you out. But we heard this week that we have to do a major writing project on John Bunyan by the end of term. Have we much more to do?' Amy asked.

'How long is a pieces of string?' Andy said 'As long as you need. I would think we have to say a bit more about Bunyan's beliefs, and his pastoral and preaching work after he came out of prison, and then talk briefly about his final visit to London. That should see us done and dusted,' Andy said. 'See you next week!'

chapter twelve

JOHN BUNYAN—PREACHER AND PASTOR

Amy's opening remarks on her next Saturday visit were to Andy's liking. He was always mildly irritated and embarrassed when his visitors went on about his illness. He hated fuss.

'Andy Pandy, does John Bunyan get out of jail today? Does the Tink from the Clink become the Tink out of Clink?!'

'Yes and Yes, Amy, Andy said. 'And I'll tell you an even more surprising thing!'

'What's that, Andy?'

'He is made the official Pastor of the Bedford congregation BEFORE he gets out of clink!

'On 11 April 1670, the Conventicle Act was re-enacted and the authorities really got tough on all unauthorised meetings. Then in April 1971, Parliament was prorogued (dismissed without being dissolved), and the Bedford congregation voted to have a settled pastor. They reported on 21 January 1672:

'After much seeking God by prayer and sober conference formerly had, the congregation did at this meeting with joint consent, signified by solemn lifting up of their hands, call forth and appoint our brother John Bunyan to the pastoral office or eldership. And he accepting thereof gave up himself to serve Christ and His Church in that charge, and received of the elders the right hand of fellowship.' It was a kind of Declaration of Faith and Hope that he would soon get out of jail....'

'And did he?'

'On March 15 1672 King Charles II issued his Declaration of Indulgence, in which he suspended all penal laws against Non-Conformists, whether Protestant or Roman Catholic. Although he was free to come and go as a preacher from March at least, and was licensed as a Congregational preacher on 9 May, his name wasn't listed on a General Pardon to prisoners until 13 September. After his release, he was to live through some troubled years in England—the Popish Plot, the death of King Charles II, and the events surrounding the succession of James II, who as Duke of York had declared himself as a Roman Catholic.

'So John Bunyan found himself, officially, Pastor of the congregation which had been led by his beloved friend John Gifford from 1650. To show the breadth of his sympathies, there is an entry in the Baptismal Register of the parish church of St Cuthbert, Bedford, for his son, Joseph, in November 1672.' The Congregationalists claim him as one of theirs, yet he says: 'I own water baptism to be God's ordinance, but I make no idol of it.'

Amy asked 'Did Bunyan make any special changes in church worship?'

Andy responded with some gusto:

'Well, how about hymn-singing, for a start. The sixteenth-century Reformation had used hymns set to popular tunes as a means of infiltrating popular culture with the Gospel. It's a sound idea! Just think how hard it is to remember French grammar, but how easy it is to remember French songs!'

'Thomas Sternhold translated metrical psalms for singing. William Tyndale wanted ploughboys to sing Psalms at work, and Miles Coverdale had a hymnbook, published in 1539, burnt by order of HenryVIII.

'The practice of hymn-singing had been extended in the seventeenth century. John Bunyan not only used hymns in the Bedford congregation, but he also wrote them. He saw popular culture as an ally. 'Pilgrim's Progress' is full of music and dancing, and 'Who would true valour see', and the Shepherd Boy's song 'He that is down need fear no fall' from Pilgrim's Progress Part II became standard hymns in the church's repertoire for centuries. There is some evidence that in order to prevent quarrels, Bunyan had hymn-singing at the start of services, so that dyed-in-the-wool Psalm-singers could come later!

'Was he kept busy after he came out of prison?'

'During the period after his release, John Bunyan preached widely, pastored faithfully, and wrote energetically. He was forty-three years old, and felt he had to make up for lost time! He produced a book of Gospel appeal based on John 6 v 37, called 'Come, and Welcome, to Jesus Christ' in 1681. He produced 'The Life and Death of Mr. Badman' in 1680, and 'The Holy War' in 1682. Scholars rate 'The Holy War' next to 'Grace Abounding' and 'Pilgrim's Progress' as Bunyan's best works.

'The congregations who knew him before imprisonment were delighted to welcome him back, and he travelled widely on horseback. His tinker's business was totally run down, and he had to have it as a secondary interest, he was so much in demand as a preacher. He got to London several times, and had joyful reunions with his great friend, John Owen, a preacher and writer, and former Dean of Christ Church and Vice-Chancellor of Oxford University. John Owen also served in high office in Cromwell's Government. John Owen loved to hear John Bunyan preach, and told Charles II he would gladly give all his academic learning in exchange for the tinker's skill in touching the hearts of his hearers. (This shows, incidentally, what a widespread reputation Bunyan had as a preacher, that the King asked John Owen for an opinion.)'

'John Bunyan obviously was very limited in his education,' Amy said. 'Who influenced him most?'

'Amy, he was a man of the Bible, first and foremost. The scholars are amazed at his grasp of the Bible, which shows in his earliest writings, even when he is busily tearing strips off the Quakers and the Ranters!

The tattered copy of Luther's commentary on the Letter to the Galatians deeply affected him. He saw across the centuries that Martin Luther and he were 'soul-mates.' He shared Luther's view that 'good works do not make a good man, but a good man does good works.' Like Luther he became convinced that 'A Christian is not he who is without sin, but he to whom God does not impute (reckon) sin, because of the grace of Christ and His death on the Cross for our sins.' He learned from Luther the clear division between law and grace, and the need to live a holy life after conversion.

'When he managed to buy 'Foxe's Book of Martyrs' in prison, that had a great effect on him, as did the two books his first wife (Mary?) got from her dad. The author of 'The Plaine Man's Pathway', Arthur Dent, influenced Bunyan in his attitude to riches and poverty, and in the need for good Christian behaviour in all our relationships. Similarly, Lewis Bayly, the author of 'The Practice of Piety', who said: 'For the most part, the poor receive the Gospel...not many mighty, not many noble are called...few rich men shall be saved.' Bunyan would agree with Bayly and Paul, on that. John Owen's influence was significant, but came later on in his life. John Owen often invited Bunyan to preach in his congregation at Moorfields, and probably introduced Bunyan to his publisher, Nathaniel Ponder, with significant results for the circulation of 'Pilgrim's Progress.'

'To return to what I said, Bunyan loved the Bible above any other book. The Bible was his basis for life and hope, and the measure of all life and behaviour. He would have been lost without it. Like so many Christians before and after him, God's kindness shown to him in and through Scripture made him biased in its favour, so that he accepts its authority even when he cannot find rational explanations of some of its difficult sections or texts.'

'Andy, I can see you are tiring,' said Amy, and we'll look forward to hearing how the tinker ended his life...Next time! Au revoir, and God bless!'

chapter thirteen

THE PILGRIM GOES HOME!

Amy zipped her anorak right to the top and bent into the wind as she struggled through the windswept streets of Leahaven for what could be her final visit to Andy's home.

'Some day today, Amy,' Andy greeted her, 'and I think it's supposed to be summer. Did you hear about the Englishman who went in for a haircut, and missed the summer? Is it true some British birds fly upside down so that they don't have to look at the misery?'

Amy was keen to push on with John Bunyan's story, so she got on to the subject as soon as possible.

'It must have been great to have such a sense of freedom after all those years in jail, Andy. How did John Bunyan react?'

Andy took up the story. 'First of all, Amy, he felt a bit like King Charles II. He didn't want to 'go on his travels again'—especially into jail! But he wanted to be prepared for anything, especially as the Bedford Church experienced difficulties and hostility during the 1680s. Sometimes they met in secret, and John Bunyan decided to take steps on behalf of his dear wife, Elizabeth. He drew up a 'Deed of Gift' on behalf of Elizabeth, in his own handwriting, and had it witnessed by four church members. The document is dated 23 December 1685. One of my sources contained a facsimile copy of the document, which says:

'To all people to whom this present writing shall come, I, John Bunyan, of the parish of St Cuthberts, in the town of Bedford, brazier, send greeting. Know ye that I, the said John Bunyan, as well for and in natural consideration of the natural affection and love which I have and bear unto my well-beloved wife, Elizabeth, as also for divers other good causes and considerations me at this present especially moving, have given and granted...all and singular my goods, chattels, debts, ready money, plate, rings, household stuff, apparel, utensils, brass, pewter, bedding and all other substance whatsoever....'
Although the document was not a will, Bunyan was trying to make provision for Elizabeth in case he would be arrested. He was trying to prevent his possessions being seized to pay fines or court costs. Elizabeth seemed not to know that this document existed, for it was found hidden in the bricks of the chimney when his house was being demolished in 1838, one hundred and fifty years after his death. Tourists who visit the Bunyan Museum in Bedford can see it for themselves.'

'Was he worried about becoming ill? Was that the reason for drawing up the 'Deed of Gift?' Amy asked.

'I am sure his health was an important but secondary reason. We have so 'soft' a life-style, with our carpets, instant hot water and central heating, that we can hardly imagine what it was like to go through many winters without heat, sleeping on straw on a stone floor, and so on. Although he was physically fit and robust when he was a young man, the years in prison took their toll. From time to time, John Bunyan complains about what we would call 'chest and lung' problems.

His preaching travels also would give him a tiring and punishing schedule, and there were pastoral 'spin-offs.' As a result of his preaching and Christian experience, he would be called on as a wise counsellor to help people find solutions to their problems. In his writings, the apostle Paul talks about 'the care of all the churches', and Bunyan would appreciate what his guide and mentor Martin Luther said in his Commentary on Galatians 6 verse 3 'Bear one another's burdens, and so fulfil the law of Christ'—'Christians need broad shoulders and mighty bones to bear the burden.'

'During the summer of 1688, a neighbour came to John Bunyan in a state of anxiety, and asked John to help resolve a disagreement between him and his father. John Bunyan promised to visit the father, who lived in Reading, Berkshire, and do what he could to help. He decided to fit the visit in with his plans for a preaching tour, heading for London. Bunyan had not been feeling well since spring, and Elizabeth was concerned about his health. John Bunyan insisted he would be alright, and had a successful outcome to his meeting with the angry father, which would hopefully achieve reconciliation between father and son. John set out for London on 16 August, and had to ride through very stormy weather and a torrential downpour of rain. He should have stopped and taken shelter somewhere, but decided to complete his journey, and arrived at the home of his friend John Strudwick, a grocer, in Snow Hill, Holborn, London. Bunyan was exhausted, shivering with cold, and soaked to the skin. He was given some tender loving care, hot herbal drinks, and insisted by Sunday that he was fit to preach. His last sermon was on the text in John 1 verse 13: 'Which were born, not of blood, nor of the will of the flesh, nor of the will of man, but of God.' He preached it at the meeting house in Petticoat Lane, Whitechapel, in the East End of London.

On the following Tuesday John developed pneumonia and was confined to bed with a raging fever. Unfortunately, his friends did not realise how serious his illness was, and they didn't let Elizabeth know, or ask her to come, although John was quite ill for ten days. Friday 31 August 1688 opened with a thunderstorm, breaking the spell of oppressive, humid weather. Some friends gathered round John near sunset, and when they asked him what they could do for him, he said quietly: 'Brothers, I desire nothing more than to be with Christ, which is far better.' He sat up in bed momentarily, stretched out his arms, and cried triumphantly 'Take me for I come to Thee'. That is how the Pilgrim got to the City of Gold, Amy. A large number of people came to see his body being buried on 3 September 1688 in Bunhill Fields in the City of London, in the family tomb of the Strudwicks. Some other well-known characters were also buried in that cemetery, including John Owen, Isaac Watts the hymnwriter, Daniel Defoe, author of another famous book, 'Robinson Crusoe', and Susannah Wesley, mother of the famous Methodist preachers John and Charles.'

'Andy, thank you, thank you, thank you!' Amy said, and much to his embarrassment threw her arms around him and gave him a big kiss.

'If it hadn't been for you, I would never have known the wonderful tinker of Bedford!'

'And thank you, thank you, thank you, Amy!' Andy looked as if he didn't know where to put himself. 'Because you got me to start this study, I have become a Pilgrim myself! And I have good news for you! God is good! I am able to have something which Mr. Bunyan could not have....We got word today that I am going in for a lung transplant very soon—next week, in fact! I could be much better in the not-too-distant future.'

Amy walked slowly home, so grateful for all she had learned from Andy, and wondering what Saturday afternoons would be like until Andy got back home.

BOOKS CONSULTED

John Bunyan Choice Works. Second Series Milner and Co., Halifax.

John Bunyan Grace Abounding to the Chief of Sinners.
Modern English version. Moody Press. Chicago. 1959

John Bunyan 'Journey to Hell', formerly 'The Life and Death of Mr.
Badman' Whitaker House, New Kensington, Pa 15608. 1999.

John Bunyan. Pilgrim's Progress. Ed. by Rhona Pipe.
Hodder and Stoughton, London. 1988.

John Bunyan Pilgrim's Progress, retold by Geraldine
McCaughrean. Hodder Headline Ltd. London. 1999.

John Bunyan The Pilgrim's Progress and Other Works.
Ed. GB Cheever. William McKenzie, Glasgow. 1861.

Maurice Ashley Charles I and Oliver Cromwell.
Methuen. London. 1987.

Robert Ashton The English Civil War. Conservation and Revolution.
1603-1649. Weidenfeld and Nicolson. London. 2nd Edition 1989.

Roland H Bainton The History of Christianity.
Nelson. London. 1964.

Martyn Bennett. The English Civil War.
Longman, Harlow, Essex. 1995.

The British Medical Association Complete Family Health Encyclopedia.
Ed. Tony Smith. Dorling Kindersley Ltd. London 1990.

Vera Britten In the Steps of John Bunyan.
Rich and Cowan. London 1950. Reprinted 1970.

John Brown. John Bunyan, His Life, Times and Work.
Wm Isbister Ltd. London 1885.

Rodney Castleden. The Concise Encyclopedia of World History.
Parragon Book Service. London. 1994.

Stephen Friar. The Batsford Companion to Local History.
BT Batsford Ltd. London 1991.

Richard Greaves. John Bunyan.
Sutton Courteney Press, Abingdon, Berkshire. 1969.

Gwilym O Griffith. John Bunyan.
Hodder and Stoughton. London. 1928.

Frank Mott Harrison. John Bunyan. A Story of His Life.
Banner of Truth Trust. London. 1964.

Christopher Hill. A Turbulent, Seditious and Fractious People. John
Bunyan and His Church. 1628-1688. Oxford University Press. 1988.

Christopher Hill. Society and Puritanism in Pre-Revolutionary England.
Secker and Warburg. London. 1964.

Lion Handbook. The History of Christianity.
Lion Publishing. Oxford. 1990 (revised edition).

Marcus L Loane. Makers of Puritan History.
Baker Book House. Grand Rapids, Michigan. 1961.

Diana Newton. Papists, Protestants and Puritans. 1559-1714.
Cambridge University Press. 1998.

The Oxford Dictionary of the Christian Church. Ed FL Cross
Oxford University Press. London. 1958.

The Oxford English Reference Dictionary. Ed Judy Pearsall and Bill Trumble. Revised 2nd edition. Oxford University Press. 2002.

JI Packer. Among God's Giants.
Kingsway Publications, Eastbourne. 1991.

Mary J Packham. Goodnight James
Waddie and Co.Ltd. Edinburgh. 1986.

John Pestell. Travel with John Bunyan. Exploring the world of John Bunyan. Day One. Epsom, Surrey. 2002.

Stuart Reid. All the King's Armies.
Spellmount Ltd. Staplehurst, Kent. 1998.

SOME INTERESTING DATES

1603-25	James I King of England as well as Scotland. The first Stuart King.
1618-48	The Thirty Years War
1625-40	Charles I succeeds James I
1628	Birth of John Bunyan
1629-40	Personal Rule of Charles I, without Parliament
1634-1639	Ship Money, Charles I's revenue-raising scheme
1639-40	The Bishops' War
1640	April-May: The Short Parliament
1641	November: The Long Parliament
1642-45	The Civil War
1643	Sept: Solemn League and Covenant with Scotland
1644	Nov: John Bunyan (aged 16) joins the Parliamentary Army at Newport Pagnell
1644	April: Formation of New Model Army

	June: Parliamentary victory at Battle of Naseby
1647	June: King Charles I seized July: John Bunyan demobilised August: Army occupies London
1648	Second Civil War
1649	January: Trial and Execution of King Charles I March-May: Republic established, House of Lords abolished. John Bunyan's first marriage.
1650	Compulsory attendance at parish church abolished
1651	Battle of Worcester. Charles II and Scottish Army defeated.
1653	July-Dec: Barebones Parliament. Civil Registration of births, marriages and deaths established.
1653-58	Protectorate of Oliver Cromwell
1655	Bunyan received into Bedford congregation
1656-57	Offer of Crown to Oliver Cromwell. Refused.
1658	Death of Oliver Cromwell. Succeeded by son Richard. Death of John Bunyan's first wife.
1659	Richard Cromwell abdicates. Long Parliament, and Republic restored. John Bunyan's second marriage.

1660	Mar : Long Parliament dissolved. April: Declaration of Breda April-Dec: Convention Parliament. House of Lords restored. May: Charles II accepted as King of England. Episcopacy Restored.
1660-62	Ejection of ca. 1760 ministers who would not conform to Revised Book of Common Prayer.
1661	April: Cavalier Parliament. November: Bunyan imprisoned
1662	Charles II's First Declaration of Indulgence.
1664	First Conventicle Act
1665	Five Mile Act. The Great Plague
1666	Fire of London
1667	Milton publishes 'Paradise Lost'
1670	Second Conventicle Act
1671	January: Bunyan appointed Pastor of Bedford congregation March: Charles II's Second Declaration of Indulgence.
1672	Parliament forces withdrawal of Declaration of Indulgence. Test Act. James, Duke of York, declares himself a Roman Catholic.

1676-7   Bunyan's second imprisonment.

1678   The Popish Plot

1679   Cavalier Parliament dissolved

1679-81   Three Parliaments in rapid succession
James Duke of York excluded from the succession

1685   Death of Charles II. James II succeeds
Dec: Bunyan conveys his property to his wife

1687   James II's first Declaration of Indulgence

1688   April: Second Declaration of Indulgence
August: Death of John Bunyan
November: William of Orange lands in England
James II flees to France.

1689-92   Bunyan's posthumous works published.